BUSINESS PLANS THAT WORK

A Guide for Small Business

BUSINESS PLANS THAT WORK

A Guide for Small Business

Jeffry A. Timmons
Andrew Zacharakis
Stephen Spinelli

McGraw-Hill

New York   Chicago   San Francisco   Lisbon   London   Madrid
Mexico City   Milan   New Delhi   San Juan   Seoul
Singapore   Sydney   Toronto

1 2 3 4 5 6 7 8 9 0   DOC/DOC   0 9 8 7 6 5 4

ISBN 0-07-141287-5

Printed and bound by RR Donnelley.

McGraw-Hill books are available at special quantity discounts to use as premiums and sales promotions, or for use in corporate training programs. For more information, please write to the Director of Special Sales, Professional Publishing, McGraw-Hill, Two Penn Plaza, New York, NY 10121-2298. Or contact your local bookstore.

This book is printed on recycled, acid-free paper containing a minimum of 50% recycled, de-inked fiber.

Contents

Preface

We have worked with hundreds of entrepreneurs over the years (over 75 years of combined experience) in varying capacities: as practicing entrepreneurs, professional equity investors, advisers, and board directors. Through our efforts we have come to appreciate the value of business planning. Those who argue that the business plan is time-consuming and is obsolete the moment it is complete are missing the point. The business plan isn't just a tool to raise capital; it is a process that helps entrepreneurs gain deep knowledge about their ideas. The discipline that the planning process provides helps you assess the nature of the opportunity and explore ways to execute that opportunity. Will your business model change once you start the business? Absolutely. In fact, going through the business planning process will result in modifications even before you launch the business. That doesn't mean that business planning is a wasted exercise. We guarantee that the act of business planning will save you countless hours and sums of money in false starts simply because it will help you anticipate the resources required and the pitfalls that may arise. Even though business planning can't help you anticipate every potential problem, the deep learning will more than offset the costs of writing the plan.

Book Design

This book will illustrate a proven and innovative approach to writing a business plan. Each chapter will introduce different components of the planning process. Also, each chapter will illustrate the concepts by high-lighting FireFly Toys, an actual company in the launch stage. The key feature of this section is the comments in the margins that point out various aspects of the plan that are good and others that need work. As you read through the book, you will become familiar not only with the process but also with FireFly Toys. A word of caution: Your business plan will vary from the FireFly plan in many areas. Each company has a unique story, and while there is a consistent core to the business plan process, your process will vary in terms of emphasis and the length of the various components. To drive this point home and provide another example, Appendix 3 has a dehydrated plan for a different type of company in a different type of industry that might be sent to a potential investor.

Fossa Industries is a medical device company currently in the U.S. Food and Drug Administration (FDA) approval phase. The company has been successful in raising capital during a very difficult period (after the dot-com bomb). Appendix 4 shows Powerpoint slides that are used when pitching to investors. As with the FireFly example, we use marginal comments to point out various features of the Fossa plan.

As you begin this exciting adventure in the world of entrepreneurship or as you take a second look at your current business, we hope you look at this as a *process*. The final product, a completed business plan, is one step in the journey. There are many more steps, and many more business plans will be completed; the important thing to take away from this book is the idea that the business plan process is one of learning. Going through the process helps you anticipate the future and thereby save time and money. This is a high-yield investment in your future success. Internalize this way of thinking and you will move beyond the failure rule and hit the thresholds that lead to ultimate success and return.

We hope you will find this book useful as you embark on your journey. Good luck.

1 ENTREPRENEURS CREATE THE FUTURE

We are in the midst of a silent
revolution—a triumph of the
creative and entrepreneurial
spirit of humankind throughout
the world. I believe its impact on
the 21st Century will equal or
exceed that of the Industrial
Revolution on the 19th and 20th.

Jeffry A. Timmons
The Entrepreneurial Mind, *1989*

Entrepreneurship runs deep in the American psyche. Many of to-day's heroes are celebrated for their entrepreneurial achievements. Bill Gates, Steven Jobs, Sam Walton, and Arthur Blank, among others, have created businesses that are household names (Microsoft, Apple Computer, Wal-Mart, and Home Depot). Whereas people entering the workforce in the 1960s and 1970s sought larger corporations and job security, people entering the workforce today are seeking younger, entrepreneurial firms or launching their own ventures. If America has learned anything in the last 20 years, it is that job security is a myth. To succeed, people need to be creative in designing their careers. That means seeking jobs that build your skill set and position you to start your own business at some future point. For those of you reading this book, the time may be now. You are not alone in your entrepreneurial dreams. Twenty-two million of your fellow Americans are in the process of launching a business or own a business less than four years old. Ultimately, the most rewarding and satisfying careers are those which are created for oneself; create a company rather than a job.

Babson College, along with the London Business School, has spearheaded the Global Entrepreneurship Monitor (GEM) project, which tracks the rate of entrepreneurship across 40 countries. Entrepreneurship is defined as any attempt to create a new business. The best estimates of the entrepreneurial activity rate for adults age 18 to 74 in 1993 was around 4 percent. After peaking at around 16.7 percent[1] during the Internet boom in 2000, the rate dropped to 10.5 percent in 2002, which was still over twice the level of activity since 1993. In 2003, the activity rate improved to 11.9%.[2] However, not every entrepreneur succeeds in launching a business, and only 40 percent of launched businesses survive longer than six years. This book is designed to help you get beyond the prelaunch stage, navigate the new business stage, and ultimately grow into a sustainable enterprise that is both personally and financially rewarding.

This chapter provides a background on the state of entrepreneurship in the United States, showing which firms beat the failure rule and why. The chapter continues with an overview of attributes that successful people possess. Next, the chapter illustrates when ideas are opportunities and provides a framework (the Timmons Model).

Entrepreneurship in America

To understand what works and what doesn't work, it is useful to examine who entrepreneurs are. We can think of entrepreneurs as falling into different categories based on the stage of development of their businesses. *Nascent entrepreneurs* are individuals in the prelaunch mode. They have yet to pay themselves or any employees a salary. *New business owners* are entrepreneurs who have paid salaries and whose business is less than four years old—a critical phase in entrepreneurship. Once

---

[1]Since 1999 we have defined entrepreneurial active adults as 18 to 64 years old, as many people beyond age 64 years are retired.

[2]To learn more about the GEM project and read past reports, go to http://www.gem-consortium.org/default.asp.

the business has survived and reached positive cash flow—usually by the fourth year at the latest—the business is closing in on being a sustainable enterprise and the entrepreneur's task moves toward building on the foundation she has laid.

Nascent Entrepreneurs

Nascent entrepreneurs are individuals who report that they are taking steps[3] toward launching a business but have not yet paid themselves or anybody else in the organization a salary or wages. In 2002, 7 percent of the adult population (or 1 in 14 adults) was in the process of launching a business. Men are more likely to be nascent entrepreneurs than women are (1.5 men for every woman), but the rate of women becoming entrepreneurs has been accelerating in the last decade. Entrepreneurs are people of all ages, but most are between 18 and 44. They tend to be college-educated, but there are many who have not finished high school. As you can see from the demographics, entrepreneurship isn't confined to highly educated men but is an encompassing phenomenon in the United States. There are times in a person's life when it is more likely that he will pursue entrepreneurship (the midthirties), but exceptions to that rule abound (Colonel Sanders was in his sixties when he launched Kentucky Fried Chicken, and Bill Gates was a teenager when he launched Microsoft). We often describe entrepreneurship as the art and craft of the creative, the unexpected, and the exceptional. The inspiration, if you will, may strike at any time in your life as long as you are open to seeing new opportunities.

Not all nascent entrepreneurs launch their businesses successfully. Many discover in this prelaunch stage that the business isn't viable for any number of reasons. For instance, the opportunity may not be large enough for a person to leave an existing job. You need to be confident that the business can grow to a level where you will be able to pay yourself a good salary compared with what you are making now. Moreover, you must recognize that it typically takes two or more years to approach revenue figures that make that earning potential possible. There are opportunity costs to pursuing an entrepreneurial venture. Other flaws may become apparent in the prelaunch phase. You may learn that you lack

---

[3]The steps might include seeking funding, a location, or supplies and writing a business plan, among others.

the skills necessary to be successful, and so you may postpone your dream while you seek jobs that will build that skill set. Entrepreneurs invariably find it difficult to raise the necessary capital, and less determined individuals will abandon their plans.

The critical thing is the learning curve. New and old businesses make mistakes, some of which may lead to failure, but successful entrepreneurs manage mistakes better. Successful entrepreneurs recognize that learning events help them reshape the opportunity so that it better meets customers' needs. The business planning process can help you compress and create those learning curves and move from nascent entrepreneur to business owner. Business planning will save you considerable amounts of time and money by helping you understand and anticipate the obstacles that all entrepreneurs face in launching a business. In articulating in the business plan the nature of the opportunity and the way you will exploit it, you have to answer many of the real-life questions you ultimately will face in practice. Indeed, your immersion in writing a great business plan will carry over into the execution of that plan. You will build a textured awareness of the market and ways to attack it. In essence, writing a great plan provides the momentum to be a great entrepreneur, but the plan is *not* the business.

Even if you launch your business successfully, not all new business owners will survive. Traditionally, the failure rate for new businesses has progressed as follows: 23 percent fail within two years, 52 percent fail within four years, and 63 percent fail within six years. Although these numbers hold over time, they vary by industry and company type. We believe that you can move those percentages in your favor by gaining a deep understanding of your capabilities as a leader-founder, what it will take for the business to succeed, and how to create ways to make this happen. Business planning is part of that process. It is a useful tool for understanding the potential, the risks, and the payoff for a particular opportunity.

Sustainable Organizations

Who are the survivors? What new businesses ultimately make the transition into the sustainable business mode? The odds for survival and a higher level of success change dramatically if the venture reaches a critical mass of at least 10 to 20 people with $2 million to $3 million in revenues and is pursuing opportunities with growth potential. One-year survival rates for new firms jump from approximately 78 percent for firms with up to 9 employees to approximately 95 percent for firms with 20 to 99 employees. After four years, the survival rate jumps from approximately 35 to 40 percent for firms with fewer than 19 employees to about 55 percent for firms with 20 to 49 employees.

Growth is implicit in entrepreneurship. The entrepreneur's goal often includes expansion and the building of long-term value and durable cash flow streams. However, it takes a long time for new companies to become established and grow. Historically, two of every five small firms founded survived six or more years but few achieved growth during the first four years.[4] That study also found that survival rates more than double for firms that grow, and the earlier in the life of the business that growth occurs, the higher the chance of survival is.[5] The 2003 *Inc.* magazine 500 exemplifies this, with an average growth rate of 1312%,[6] despite a slow economy. The lesson from these studies is that entrepreneurs need to think big. Don't create a job; build a business.

Another notable exception to the failure rule involves businesses that have attracted start-up financing from successful private venture capital companies. While venture-backed firms account for a very small percentage of new firms each year (in 2000 only 5,557 companies received venture capital[7]), 238 of 414[8] initial public offerings (IPOs) in 2000, or 57 percent, had venture backing. An IPO is an important milestone in the development of a company as it gives it the capital to grow into a major industry player. Clearly, venture capital is not essential to a start-up. Among the companies that made the 2003 *Inc.* magazine 500, only 2 percent raised venture capital.[9] However, companies with venture capital support fair better overall. Only 46 companies with venture capital declared bankruptcy or became defunct in 2000.[10] This is less than 1 percent of companies that received venture capital in that year.

---

[4]Bruce D. Phillips and Bruce A. Kirchhoff, "An Analysis of New Firm Survival and Growth," in *Frontiers in Entrepreneurship Research: 1988,* pp. 266–267.
[5]This reaffirms the exception to the failure rule noted above and in the original edition of *New Venture Creation* (Timmons) in 1977.
[6]Mike Hoffman, "The Big Picture," *Inc.,* Fall 2003, vol. 25, issue 11.
[7]Venture Economics, http://www.ventureeconomics.com/vec/stats/2001q2/us.html, July 30, 2001.
[8]"Aftermarket at a Glance" *IPO Reporter,* December 10, 2001, and "IPO Aftermarket," *Venture Capital Journal,* December 2001.
[9]Mike Hoffman, "The Big Picture," *Inc.,* 2003, vol. 25, issue 11, p. 89.
[10]*VentureXpert,* Thompson Financial Data Services, 2001.

These compelling figures have led some to conclude that there is a threshold core of 10 percent to 15 percent of new companies that will become the winners in terms of size, job creation, profitability, innovation, and potential for harvesting (and thereby realize a capital gain). As you plan your business, think of ways to attain these threshold milestones. Does this mean you have to be a venture capital–backed firm to succeed and create wealth? We think not. However, the lessons delivered in this book reflect the high standards of content, format, and presentation that venture capital firms require. By understanding due diligence, intimate involvement in planning, and the intricacies of your deal, you will increase your odds of launching and sustaining a new venture.

Lessons from the Dot-Com Meltdown

Although failure rates seem to be relatively stable, there are instances where they become more severe. Furthermore, ignoring the fundamental lessons of entrepreneurship can lead to failure even if a venture achieves many of the threshold criteria discussed above. Take the Internet boom and subsequent bust. The creation rate during the late 1990s was phenomenal, but by 2000 the failure rate had exploded. Through the third quarter of 2002, nearly 900 Internet companies had shut down or declared bankruptcy.[11] Several lessons can be learned from the Internet debacle.

1. Entrepreneurship Is Hard Work that Requires Both Creativity and Rigor

During the boom, entrepreneurs had visions of easy money and quick success. Television, newspapers, and magazines highlighted stories of instant billionaires. It seemed that all that was necessary was to be young, create a concept with the term *Internet* in it, and go out and seek start-up capital. The idea didn't have to be original (how many Internet toy companies, pet supply companies, and electronic gadget companies were there?); the goal was to spend as much money as possible and hope that it led to an impenetrable market share. Fast growth in Internet traffic led to public offerings that created instant paper billionaires and funneled more capital for a company to spend foolishly.

---

[11]www.webmergers.com. "Q3 Report: Shutdowns Down Sharply from 2001."

What we learned (or relearned) is that entrepreneurship isn't about market share; it is about a strong business model. That means *profits*. You can't buy your customers forever or expect undying loyalty just because you gave customers a good deal. You need to have a product or service that customers truly value, something for which they will pay a premium. In other words, your product and supporting service need to be some combination of better, cheaper, and faster. We should pause for a moment and explain what we mean by "cheaper." Some readers might misconstrue this as meaning that your product should be priced lower than the competition. While this might be a sound strategy in some cases, most new companies don't have the economics to deliver a lower-priced product effectively. Instead, "cheaper" may mean that you have a cost advantage that adds value for your customers. For instance, Dell's production process is cheaper than that of many of its competitors because Dell doesn't build up large inventories that are stockpiled at retailers in advance of a sale. Instead, Dell adds tremendous value to end users because it can configure a computer the way customers want and have it delivered to their homes or businesses in a matter of days. Dell effectively eliminates the middleman. To develop an advantage that is some combination of better, faster, and cheaper, entrepreneurs need to understand customers and be able to adapt their businesses to serve customers better or they will face quick extinction.

The business planning process is one of learning. It is a disciplined approach in which you ask questions, seek answers, and plan for increasingly demanding market tests. Deep understanding and the ability to adapt improve your chances of success. The business planning process helps you move beyond the nascent entrepreneurial stage and survive the new business ownership phase.

2. Too Much Money Is as Dangerous as Too Little

Failed entrepreneurs often cite a lack of capital as the primary reason for a firm's demise. The opposite was true in the Internet boom. Venture capitalists eager to invest large sums of money with the prospects of quick liquidity via IPOs poured more money into Internet companies than those companies could digest. At the peak in early 2000, venture capitalists were pumping $8 million to $15 million per round of investment into early-stage deals and a whopping $22 million[12] per round into later-stage

---

[12]VentureOne.

deals. Expected to spend that money, many Internet entrepreneurs spent foolishly in vain efforts to capture market share. Boo.com spent $130 million in seven months to launch a fashion website and failed. Webvan blew over $800 million and then failed. The excess money insulated those companies from the market test for a while. With huge war chests of cash, those companies could sell their products or provide their services at a loss and never really know if they could command a price high enough to generate a profit. Market share was all that mattered because there was going to be some investor (usually the public market) who would pay more than the company was worth. Then, conceivably, the entrepreneur and the early investors could get their money out, plus huge returns. Ultimately, those companies destroyed wealth and few entrepreneurs enjoyed the highly publicized short-term gains. Toby Lenk, the founder of eToys, was worth $850 million (on paper) the day after his company went public. In part to set an example and in part because selling a large chunk of his shares would have hurt the overall value of his company, Lenk held almost all his shares until the company went bankrupt.[13]

The key is to get enough money to get started but not so much that your business is insulated from market tests. It is critical to learn early whether your product or service has the potential to earn profits. Your venture needs to answer several questions in the early iterations of growth: Will the customer pay enough for the product so that the firm can be profitable? Will the customer stay loyal to your company or shop for the best price? How much will it cost to capture the customer in the first place? If your entrepreneurial venture is on a tight budget, you learn the answers to these questions quickly. You then have time to adapt the business so that it answers those questions in the affirmative. Business planning helps you define milestones you need to achieve on your journey toward a sustainable business. Once you identify these milestones, business planning helps you assess how much capital you need to achieve them and when you should raise that capital. Devise your funding strategy around those key milestones. For example, in developing a prototype, you may be able to finance it with your own resources, such as your time and small infusions of your personal cash. After you have a prototype, the next milestone may be to produce and sell your product

---

[13]M. Sokolove, "How to Lose $850 Million—and Not Really Care." *New York Times Magazine*, June 9, 2000, pp. 64–67.

or service. This may require getting investment from friends and family members. Tying your capital needs to milestones helps you test the concept, see if it passes, and then move toward the next milestone.

3. The First Mover's Advantage Is an Urban Legend

Having worked with numerous entrepreneurs and student entrepreneurs, we hear over and over that "our company will have a first mover's advantage." Often that is the sole critical assumption on which the entrepreneurs base their competitive advantage. The truth is that the first mover's advantage rarely works in isolation from other competitive advantages. Example upon example illustrates that the first to market is rarely the industry leader in the long run. Apple had the first PDA, the Newton. Visicalc had the first spreadsheet but was supplanted by Lotus 123, which was supplanted by Microsoft Excel. Being first to market doesn't mean you will own the market.

True competitive advantage can be summed up as a combination of faster, cheaper, and better. Most often this occurs within a niche in a larger industry. Take Home Depot. It revolutionized the hardware industry by offering a warehouse of goods. That allowed Home Depot to offer better prices because it could get volume discounts from its suppliers. That power increased as suppliers realized that they could move a lot of product though the Home Depot distribution channel. The suppliers accepted lower margins on their products. Home Depot supplemented that advantage by hiring skilled associates who could answer do-it-yourselfers' questions. Free clinics on common projects, such as building a deck or installing a ceiling fan, supplemented that expertise. That gave Home Depot a "better" product. Finally, customers knew that Home Depot would have what they needed when they wanted it. Home Depot enabled its customers to do their projects "faster." Thus, Home Depot built a powerful competitive advantage based on better, cheaper, and faster.

Not every entrepreneur aspires to the size and scale of Home Depot. Even smaller companies need to think about their competitive advantage. For example, if you plan to start a restaurant, you might target higher-quality food and atmosphere as your advantage. Based on the traffic, the competition, and other factors in your geographic target, you may build a sustainable competitive advantage. The Blue Ginger in Wellesley, Massachusetts, has such an advantage. Ming Tsai, the nationally known chef, is the restaurant's founder. Sure, the food is excellent, but Ming Tsai has a reputation that is strengthened by his television show and by constant exposure in local and national media. People want to be part of the Ming Tsai experience.[14]

The goal of this book is to improve your odds through deep learning. The place to begin is your personal goals.

Understanding Yourself

The first step in the entrepreneurial process is to understand your goals and aspirations. Ask yourself the following questions:

1. What are my career goals?
2. How does an entrepreneurial endeavor help me achieve these goals?
3. What skills do I need to develop to be successful?

Entrepreneurship isn't about making money (although that often comes); it is about achieving self-actualization. Entrepreneurs view their ventures as their "babies." The analogy is strong and powerful. Entrepreneurs nurture their businesses in the early years, helping them grow and mature, often with the goal of having the business outlive them. In a sense, a business is a form of immortality. Many of the largest businesses in the country are privately held family businesses that pass from generation to generation. Coors Beer, Perdue Chicken, and the Lego Company are just a sampling of family-owned firms that survived their founders. So what does it take to be successful?

The first step is to assess what you want to achieve in the long run. We all have to work to support ourselves and our families. Entrepreneurship can be an attractive alternative to the traditional job. But just as you set goals in a traditional job (annual performance reviews), you should set goals for an entrepreneurial career. The goals should be both personal and professional, and you need to understand the trade-offs between the two. For example, many people claim that they are pursuing entrepreneurship to be their own boss. Entrepreneurs are far from independent and have to serve many masters and constituencies, including partners, investors, customers, suppliers, creditors, employees, families,

---

[14]For more on Ming, see www.ming.com.

and those involved in social and community obligations. Entrepreneurs, however, can make free choices of whether, when, and what they care to respond to. Moreover, it is extremely difficult, and rare, to build a business beyond $1 million to $2 million in sales single-handedly. Thus, the trade-off is that to be successful you have to recognize who are the important stakeholders, although you do have final say.

Other people pursue entrepreneurship to set their own hours. The underlying implication is that you can work fewer than the standard 40 hours a week that you might have to work in a corporate job. The reality is that to start a successful, growing venture (one that has the potential to be a sustainable ongoing concern) you probably will exceed 40 hours a week every week. The typical mantra of entrepreneurs is that they get to "work any 80 hours a week they want." You must understand the trade-offs going into an entrepreneurial career, because if you are surprised by the level of commitment required, you're more likely to fail.

Surprisingly, the primary motive that drives most people to entrepreneurship isn't the opportunity to become incredibly wealthy. Entrepreneurs seeking high-potential ventures are driven more by building enterprises and realizing long-term capital gains than by instant gratification through high salaries and perks. A sense of personal achievement and accomplishment, feeling in control of their own destinies, and realizing their visions and dreams are also powerful motivators. Money is viewed as a tool and a way to keep score.

If these motivators ring true to you, entrepreneurship may be the way to achieve your goals. It may be hard to envision how an entrepreneurial endeavor will help you achieve your goals unless you have been involved in previous start-ups. Business planning can help you visualize how entrepreneurship may help you achieve those goals. Business planning is nothing more than sophisticated scenario analysis. You will work through identifying the opportunity, understanding who your customer is, and figuring out how to reach that customer. Furthermore, you will see what can be. If you succeed in implementing your vision, business planning will help you imagine the future. You will get a sense of how the business might grow. Specifically, your financial pro forma statements will suggest the upside potential of a successful venture.[15]

---

[15]We will cover financial projections in great detail later in the book. It is important to note that projections are best guesses and become less accurate the farther out one goes, but they can give a sense of what can be if you identify an opportunity and execute it.

Finally, business planning will help you identify what skills are necessary to implement the business successfully. You probably will not possess all those skills. As was stated earlier, most successful ventures are launched by teams, meaning that others fill the gaps in your skills. However, you need enough skills to be credible as a lead entrepreneur. You need to have something special, whether it is technical wizardry or business acumen, that can draw others to join you in your quest. One of the first market tests all entrepreneurs confront is whether they can attract other core team members to join them. Again, the business plan will help you define what attributes those people should possess.

As we have worked with entrepreneurs over the years, we have noticed an internal drive that successful entrepreneurs possess. For that matter, it seems that people who are successful in any context possess certain attributes. One of the authors has pulled out five key ones that he shares with all the students and entrepreneurs he works with, called Zach's Star of Success.

Zach's Star of Success

Zach's Star of Success captures many of the attributes that lead to entrepreneurial success. The star progresses clockwise, starting with "knowledge." Whether one is pursuing an entrepreneurial career or a more traditional Fortune 500 career or indeed any profession, the five points of success define the key attributes people need to develop or possess in order to succeed.

Knowledge

To be successful, people need knowledge. As the late Herbert Simon, Nobel Prize winner from Carnegie Mellon University, noted, it takes 10 years and 50,000 chunks of knowledge to become expert in any area.[16] According to Simon, experts recognize patterns that can be transformed

---

[16]H. A. Simon, "What We Know about the Creative Process." In R. Kuhn (ed.), *Frontiers in Creative and Innovative Management*. Cambridge, MA: Ballinger, 1985, pp. 3–20.

from one situation to another. Their unique ability to combine those patterns in creative ways gives them an advantage in any domain in which they participate. For example, an expert chess player identifies patterns based on the current board setup and knows what moves to make next. Likewise, expert entrepreneurs see patterns in the environment and identify combinations that allow them to enter and compete in a marketplace.

It is not surprising, then, to see that many entrepreneurs launch businesses in domains where they have experience. For example, Jeff Hawkins and Donna Dubinsky worked together at Palm Computing, the company that developed the Palm Pilot. Hawkins and Dubinsky subsequently left and founded Handspring, a competitor that quickly gained market share. What happens if you don't have directly relevant experience? What if you are young or are changing industries? In such cases, it is critical to build a team to complement the entrepreneur's skill set.

Network

A powerful way to gain that knowledge is through networking. The broader one's network is, the more knowledge one can tap. This may take the form of adding people to your team or building what is called a virtual team. If we think of the entrepreneurial process, many start-ups require external financing. Often that money comes from family members, friends, and angels. These investors can add to your knowledge base, especially if you have strategically chosen an angel who has operating experience in your marketplace. Other members of the virtual team might include your accountant, your lawyer, suppliers, and even customers. All of them add to your knowledge and can help in other ways as well. For instance, your investors may provide leads to customers or your accountant and lawyer may provide leads to other investors.

The key to success is a larger network. The more people you know, the greater the odds are that you can tap into the right knowledge source. To that end, entrepreneurs should have a goal of meeting five or more new people a week. Furthermore, you need to maintain contact with your network on both a personal and a professional basis. People within your network are much more apt to respond quickly when you contact them. On a professional basis, it is important for entrepreneurs to send a periodic newsletter detailing the state of their progress to all current and potential stakeholders. This keeps you and your efforts fresh in the minds of your network and often spurs those people to act on your behalf. They might connect you with an investor or customer without your directly soliciting their help. As you start this business planning process, talk to as many people as you can and keep them informed of your progress.

Energy

Building knowledge and networking take energy. As Dennis Kimbro, best-selling author of *Think and Grow Rich: A Black Choice*, told faculty members and students when he visited Babson in 1999, "Successful people make the 40-hour workweek look like child's play." He later added, "If your work is your play and your play is your work, you will never work a day in your life." Launching a business takes a tremendous amount of energy. The typical entrepreneur can expect to work on average 60 hours a week or more. In reality, most entrepreneurs find that they never leave the job. Even when they are in bed or on vacation, entrepreneurs are thinking about the business. The business planning process also takes energy. A good plan takes 200 hours to complete, and that is just for the first working draft. This energy is somewhat self-sustaining if you also have the final two points on the star: commitment and passion.

Commitment

To sustain energy, one needs commitment because everyone will face difficult times. Launching a business is an emotional roller coaster. The highs are higher and the lows are lower, and they come at breakneck speed. If you are not committed to your opportunity, to your vision, it is all too easy to quit when the first low hits. You have to believe in yourself; you have to believe in your vision. Without that definiteness of purpose, you will abandon the venture when things look tough, and things will look tough at several points on the journey. Thus, you also need the final point to help sustain you.

Passion

The last and most important point of the star is *passion*. Returning to the self-actualization theme, you need to know what drives you. What are your professional and personal passions? As Dennis Kimbro says, "If nobody paid you, what would you do for free?" If you are pursuing entrepreneurship only to make money, you will lack the commitment and energy to be successful. Before starting the business plan process, dig deep and find what motivates you, what fulfills you. In other words, define your passion and make sure your proposed business incorporates that passion. The points on the star represent a way of life for a successful entrepreneur. We urge you to consider those points and incorporate into your life.

The Nature of Opportunity

Once you understand your career and entrepreneurial goals, as well as your passion, it is often easy to generate a list of several business ideas. However, not every idea (in fact, most ideas) represents a viable opportunity. By an opportunity we mean a business that can generate profits and provide attractive returns to the entrepreneurial team and the investors. Many failures can be attributed to great enthusiasm for ideas that don't have opportunity potential. Therefore, it is imperative to assess the potential characteristics of the opportunity before launching into the business plan or starting the business. The simplest, most robust means of understanding your opportunity is the Timmons' Model.[17]

The Timmons Model Basics

Sustainable success in creating a new venture is driven by a few central themes that dominate this highly dynamic entrepreneurial process:

- It is *opportunity*-driven.
- It is driven by a *lead entrepreneur* and an *entrepreneurial team*.
- It is *resource-parsimonious and creative*.
- It depends on the *fit and balance* among these factors.
- It is *integrated and holistic*.

These are the controllable components of the entrepreneurial process that can be assessed, influenced, and altered. Founders and investors focus on these forces during their careful due diligence process to analyze

---

[17]For a fuller discussion, please refer to J. Timmons and S. Spinelli, *New Venture Creation*, 6th ed. Boston: Irwin McGraw-Hill, 2003.

Exhibit 1.1 *The Timmons Model of the Entrepreneurial Process*

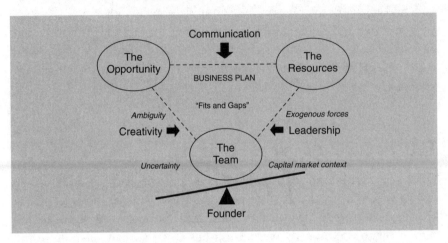

the risks and determine what changes can be made to improve a venture's chances of success, its capital requirements, the pace of growth, and other start-up strategies.

Change the Odds: Fix It, Shape It, Mold It, Make It

The driving forces underlying the creation of a successful new venture are illustrated in Exhibit 1.1. The process starts with opportunity, not money, strategy, networks, a team, or the business plan. Most genuine opportunities are much bigger than the talent or the capacity of the team or the initial resources available to the team. The role of the lead entrepreneur and the team is to juggle all these key elements in a changing environment. Think of a juggler bouncing up and down on a trampoline that is moving on a conveyor belt at unpredictable speeds and directions while trying to keep all three balls in the air. That is the dynamic nature of an early stage start-up. The business plan provides the language and code for communicating the quality of the three driving forces of the Timmons Model and their fit and balance.

Exhibit 1.1 depicts the entrepreneurial process in the Timmons Model. The shape, size, and depth of the opportunity establish the required shape, size, and depth of both the resources and the team. We have found that many people are a bit uncomfortable viewing the opportunity and the resources balanced somewhat precariously by the team.

It is especially disconcerting to some because we show the three key elements of the entrepreneurial process as circles, making the balance appear tenuous. These reactions are justified, accurate, and realistic. The entrepreneurial process is dynamic. Those who recognize the risks manage the process better and garner a bigger return.

The lead entrepreneur's job is simple enough: He must carry the deal by *taking charge of the success equation.* In this dynamic context, ambiguity and risk are your friends. Central to the homework, creative problem solving and strategizing, and due diligence that lie ahead is analyzing the fits and gaps that exist in the venture: What is wrong with this opportunity? What is missing? What good news and favorable events can happen, as well as adverse ones? What has to happen to make it attractive and a fit for me? What market, technology, competitive, management, and financial risks can be reduced or eliminated? What can be changed to make this happen? Who can change it? What are the minimal resources necessary to grow the business the farthest? Is this the right team? By implication, if one can determine these answers and make the necessary changes by figuring out how to fill the gaps, improve the fit, and attract key players who can add such value, the odds for success rise significantly. In essence, the entrepreneur's role is to manage and redefine the risk-reward equation.

The Opportunity

At the heart of the process is the opportunity. Successful entrepreneurs and investors know that a good idea is not necessarily a good opportunity. In fact, for every 100 ideas presented to investors in the form of a business plan or a proposal, usually only 1 or sometimes 2 or 3 ever get funded. Over 80 percent of those rejections occur in the first few minutes; another 10 to 15 percent occur after investors have read the business plan carefully. Fewer than 10 percent attract enough interest to merit thorough due diligence and investigation over several weeks and even months. These are very slim odds. Would-be entrepreneurs chasing ideas that are going nowhere waste countless hours and days. An important skill, therefore, as an entrepreneur or an investor is to be able to evaluate quickly whether serious potential exists and decide how much time and effort to invest.

Exhibit 1.2 summarizes the most important characteristics of good opportunities. Underlying market demand—because of the value-added

Exhibit 1.2 *The Entrepreneurial Process Is Opportunity-Driven*[18]

Market demand is a key ingredient in measuring an opportunity:
- Is customer payback less than one year?
- Do market share and growth potential equal 20 percent annual growth, and are they durable?
- Is the customer reachable?

Market structure and size:
- Emerging and/or fragmented?
- $50 million or more, with a $1 billion potential?
- Proprietary barriers to entry?

(Opportunity)

Margin analysis helps differentiate an opportunity from an idea:
- Low-cost provider (40 percent gross margin)?
- Low capital requirement versus the competition?
- Break even in 1 or 2 years?

properties of the product or service; the market's size and 20 percent or more growth potential; the economics of the business, particularly robust gross margins (40 percent or more); and free cash flow characteristics—drives the value creation potential.

In short, the greater the growth, size, durability, and robustness of the gross and net margins and the free cash flow, the greater the opportunity. The more *imperfect* the market, the greater the opportunity. The greater the rate of change, the discontinuities, and the chaos, the greater the opportunity. The greater the inconsistencies in existing service and quality and in lead times and lag times and the greater the vacuums and gaps in information and knowledge, the greater the opportunity.

Resources: Creative and Parsimonious

One of the most common misconceptions among untried entrepreneurs is that you have to have all the resources in place, especially the money,

---

[18]The durability of an opportunity is a widely misunderstood concept. In entrepreneurship, durability is when the investor gets her money back plus a market or better return on investment.

Exhibit 1.3 *Understand and Marshall Resources; Don't Be Driven by Them*

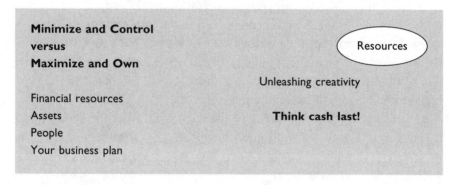

Minimize and Control
versus
Maximize and Own

Resources

Unleashing creativity

Financial resources

Assets

Think cash last!

People

Your business plan

to succeed in a venture. Thinking money first is a big mistake. Money follows high-potential opportunities conceived of and led by a strong management team. Investors have bemoaned for years the fact that there is too much money chasing too few deals. In other words, there is a shortage of quality entrepreneurs and opportunities, not of money. Successful entrepreneurs devise ingeniously creative and stingy strategies to marshal and gain control of resources (Exhibit 1.3). Investors and successful entrepreneurs often say that one of the worst things that can happen to an entrepreneur is to have *too much money too early.*

Bootstrapping is a way of life in entrepreneurial companies and can create a significant competitive advantage. Doing more with less is a powerful competitive weapon. Successful entrepreneurs try to minimize and control resources, not necessarily own them. Whether it is assets for the business, key people, the business plan, or start-up and growth capital, they *think cash last.* Such strategies have a wondrous effect on the company in two ways: a discipline of leanness is established where everyone knows that every dollar counts throughout the firm, and the principle of conserve your equity (CYE) becomes a way to maximize shareholder value.

The Entrepreneurial Team

There is little dispute today that the entrepreneurial team is a key ingredient in higher-potential ventures. Investors are captivated "by the creative brilliance of a company's head entrepreneur: a Mitch Kapor, a Steve

Jobs, a Fred Smith . . . and bet on the superb track records of the management team working as a group."[19] Venture capitalist John Doerr reaffirms the father of American venture capital General George Doriot's dictum: I prefer a grade A entrepreneur and team with a grade B idea to a grade B team with a grade A idea. Doerr stated, "In the world today, there's plenty of technology, plenty of entrepreneurs, plenty of money, plenty of venture capital. What's in short supply is great teams. Your biggest challenge will be building a great team."[20] The investor Arthur Rock articulated the importance of the team over a decade ago, putting it this way: "If you can find good people, they can always change the product. Nearly every mistake I've made has been when I picked the wrong people, not the wrong idea."[21] Finally, as we saw earlier, ventures with more than 20 employees and $2 million to $3 million in sales are much more likely to survive and prosper. In the vast majority of cases, it is very difficult to grow beyond this point without a team of two or more key contributors.

Exhibit 1.4 depicts the important aspects of the team. These teams invariably are formed and led by a very capable entrepreneurial leader whose track record exhibits both accomplishments and several qualities the team must possess. A pacesetter and culture creator, the lead entrepreneur is central to the team as both a player and a coach. The ability and skill in attracting other key management members and then building the team is one of the most valued capabilities investors look for. The founder who becomes the leader does so by building heroes in the team. A leader adapts a philosophy that rewards success and supports honest failure, shares the wealth with those who help create it, and sets high standards for both performance and conduct.

Importance of Fit and Balance

Rounding out the model of the three driving forces is the concept of fit and balance between and among these forces. Note that the team is positioned at the bottom of the triangle in the Timmons Model (Exhibit 1.1). Imagine the founder, the entrepreneurial leader of the venture, stand-

---

[19] William D. Bygrave and Jeffry A. Timmons, *Venture Capital at the Crossroads*, Boston: Harvard Business School Press, 1992, p. 8.
[20] John Doerr, *Fast Company*, February–March 1997, p. 84.
[21] Arthur Rock, "Strategy vs. Tactics from a Venture Capitalist," *Harvard Business Review*, November–December 1987, pp. 63–67.

Exhibit 1.4 *An Entrepreneurial Team Is the Key Ingredient for Success*

An entrepreneurial leader
- Learns and teaches faster and better
- Deals with adversity and is resilient
- Exhibits integrity, dependability, and honesty
- Builds entrepreneurial culture and organization
- Possesses the qualities identified in Zach's Star of Success

Team

Quality of team
- Relevant experience and track record
- Motivation to excel
- Commitment, determination, and persistence
- Tolerance of risk, ambiguity, and uncertainty
- Creativity
- Team locus of control
- Adaptability
- Opportunity obsession
- Leadership
- Communication

ing on a large ball, grasping the triangle over her head. The challenge is to balance the triangle without toppling off. This imagery is helpful in appreciating the balancing act since leader, team, and resources rarely match. When envisioning a company's future using this imagery, the entrepreneur can ask herself, What pitfalls will I encounter to get to the next boundary of success? Will my current team be large enough, or will we be over our heads if the company grows 30 percent over the next two years? Are my resources sufficient (or too abundant)? Vivid examples of failure to maintain a balance are everywhere, such as when large companies throw too many resources at a weak, poorly defined opportunity. For example, Lucent Technologies misplaced bets, and slowness to react to bandwidth demand resulted in more than a 90 percent reduction in its market capitalization.

The business plan helps you tie together the three spheres of the Timmons Model. The planning process helps you shape the opportunity and understand its full potential. Then the lead entrepreneur has a sense of what other team members are needed to fill out the venture's skill set and what resources will be needed to execute the opportunity. Examine your idea. Does it have the makings of a strong opportunity?

Scale of the Opportunity

Opportunities come in different shapes and sizes. Some opportunities are massive and may lead to entrepreneurial companies that change an industry, if not the world. For instance, through years of study we have found that the largest opportunities occur in emerging or fragmented industries. Technology such as the Internet, telecom, and biotechnology often creates new emerging industries. Within these spaces, demand exceeds supply and multiple new entrants are racing to develop the dominant platform or structure. For example, the early days of the desktop computer saw hundreds of companies competing with their product offerings. The DOS-based PCs became the dominant platform, with Apple's operating system a distant second. All other PC platforms disappeared, as well as the companies that promoted them. We have seen similar races in the Internet, telecom, and other technology arenas. These races are often about market share (and foreseeable profit). Emerging industries often have attractive gross profit margins, allowing companies to grow and adapt their business models (even though operating margins can be low or negative in the early years). As the dominant platforms develop, the industry transforms to a mature state and the gross margins decrease. Competition becomes more intense, and it is more difficult for new ventures to enter successfully. Therefore, some of the best opportunities for new ventures are in emerging industries.

Fragmented industries also provide strong opportunities. A fragmented industry is characterized by many small "mom and pop" competitors, each with a narrow geographic focus. Consider Home Depot. Before its entrance into hardware, many small mom and pop hardware stores could be found. In one of the authors' hometown just outside Boston there were three hardware stores for a town with 12,000 residents. Today only one remains, and it has affiliated with Ace Hardware. These large box stores, such as Home Depot, Wal-Mart, and Staples, have revolutionized retail by rolling up industries. Moving large volumes of product allows these entrepreneurial ventures to earn large profits even if their gross margins are less than might be experienced in emerging industries.

The size and magnitude of these opportunities draw in professional equity investors such as venture capitalists. An entrepreneur may end up with a lower percentage of the equity but, if all goes well, a much higher return. That being said, you may decide that a high-potential venture isn't for you. Your passion may reside in an opportunity that doesn't have the large upside discussed above. You may not have the skills to manage such an undertaking. You may be like the vast majority of American entrepreneurs, pursuing a "lifestyle" opportunity.

The difference between lifestyle and high-potential ventures is a function of growth potential. Examples of lifestyle firms include single establishment restaurants, dry cleaners, and self-consultant businesses. Although lifestyle firms may not make you a billionaire, many can help you become a millionaire. In fact, owning a small business such as dry cleaning has generated more millionaires than have high flying Internet start-ups. Furthermore, many lifestyle entrepreneurs transition their firms into foundation firms. An example of this might be expanding beyond a single restaurant to five or more restaurants. The size of the opportunity has become larger, as well as the potential returns. The size of the opportunity you wish to pursue is a function of your vision and career objectives, but if you are interested in a larger opportunity, keep that in mind from the outset.

This chapter has provided some background on entrepreneurship. You are about to embark on a journey that will have you joining the entrepreneurial revolution that is sweeping the country. As you begin the business planning process, keep in mind your goals and work to identify opportunities. The subsequent chapters will go into preplanning and the construction of the business plan in great detail. As you read the chapters, we will be tracking Lauren McLaughlin and her company, FireFly Toys. Put yourself in her position. Do you think she has an opportunity? Would you shape it the same way she has? Is her planning process giving her the learning she will need to be successful? Every entrepreneur will reach different conclusions, but the planning process is designed to help you pull together the information you need to make strong decisions.

2 BEFORE YOU START WRITING YOUR PLAN: ASKING THE RIGHT QUESTIONS

There are a number of activities that need work before you start writing the actual business plan. First, you do not want to write a plan for every idea you might be considering. This chapter presents the Quick Screen tool, a method that can help you evaluate several ideas quickly and decide which one is the most attractive opportunity. Once you've identified that opportunity, the next step is to detail action items you need to complete in preparation for writing the plan. We provide you with a business planning guide that will help you schedule that task. The chapter concludes with an overview of the business planning process and the three different types of plans entrepreneurs commonly use.

The Quick Screen

Time is the ultimate ally and enemy of an entrepreneur. The harsh reality is that you will not have enough time in a quarter, a year, or a decade to pursue all the ideas for businesses you and your team can think of. Perhaps the cruelest part of the paradox is that you have to find and make the time for the good ones. To complicate the paradox, we argue that *you do not have a strategy until you are saying no to lots of opportunities.* This is part of the both punishing and rewarding Darwinian act of entrepreneurship: Many will try, many will fail, some will succeed, and a few will excel. In 2000 almost 4 million new enterprises of all kinds were launched in the United States, or over 300,000 a month. Only 10 to 15 percent proved to be good opportunities that could achieve sales of $1 million or more.

Because you can't make a business plan for every idea you think has merit, it is important to screen ideas quickly to determine which ones deserve more attention. The Quick Screen is a tool that can help you weed out poor ideas quickly. Opportunities consist of the "four anchors."

1. They create or add significant value for a customer or end user.
2. They do that by solving a significant problem or meeting a significant want or need for which someone is willing to pay a premium.
3. They therefore have robust market, margin, and moneymaking characteristics: large enough ($50 million or more), high growth (20 percent or more), high margins (40 percent or more), strong and early free cash flow (recurring revenue, low assets, and working capital), and high profit potential (10 to 15 percent or more after tax) and offer attractive realizable returns for investors (25 to 30% or more IRR).
4. They are a good *fit* with the founders and the management team at the time and marketplace and with the *risk-reward* balance.

Because most sophisticated private equity investors and venture capitalists invest in only one to five out of a hundred ideas, one can see how important it is to focus on a few superior ideas. The ability to reject ideas quickly and efficiently is a very important entrepreneurial characteristic. The Quick Screen should enable you in an hour or so to conduct a preliminary review and evaluation of an idea. Unless the idea has, or you are confident it can be molded and shaped so that it has, the four anchors, you will waste a lot of time on a lower-potential idea. The next section introduces you to FireFly Toys and then illustrates the use of the Quick Screen by analyzing the FireFly opportunity. A blank copy of the Quick Screen for your own use appears in Appendix 1.

What Is FireFly Toys?

Lauren C. McLaughlin founded FireFly Toys to help children in distress. Lauren had spent her working career focusing on the needs of children, and she was attuned to the signals kids send. The original inspiration came to Lauren as she boarded an airplane. Lauren noticed a child sitting by herself (there didn't appear to be a parent). Lauren speculated that the child was from a divorced family and probably was traveling between parents. In any event, the child seemed afraid. What would ease the child's concern? How could the child be comforted? The flight attendants were busy getting ready for takeoff. Children are trained not to talk to strangers. Hence, the child sat there alone and nervous. Lauren thought the child needed something to occupy her, to provide comfort and security in an uncertain situation. This led Lauren to her initial idea: a plush toy. She knew from her experience working with children that kids under age 10 often have a favorite object, a stuffed animal or a security blanket, that they like to have close when they are upset or unsettled. The question in Lauren's mind was how to make this idea into a business.

A few years before the airline flight Lauren was contemplating going back to college and getting an MBA. Lauren had graduated from Vassar College in Poughkeepsie, New York, majoring in health issues for children. Her first job after graduation was working for a girl's orphanage in Ecuador. After a year in South America Lauren moved to San Francisco and took a job with the YWCA. During her tenure Lauren launched a Teen Women Entrepreneurs Program, worked at a runaway shelter, and developed theater workshops for children in juvenile delinquent programs. All those experiences added to Lauren's understanding of the difficulties children face. Although she loved her work, Lauren was frustrated by the lack of funding for the nonprofit. Several of her pet programs were on the cutting block. She felt that there had to be a better way to help children without being at the mercy of philanthropists. Maybe an MBA would help her identify a better way.

Lauren was interested in becoming an entrepreneur. After all, she reasoned, running a successful nonprofit was entrepreneurial. Lauren became intrigued with Babson College as she explored MBA programs. Babson consistently had been ranked as the number one MBA program for training entrepreneurs. She read about the Hatchery program where students could establish an office to operate a business while completing a degree. The Hatchery program provides students with peer support (other entrepreneurs in the launch or early days of building a new business worked side by side and shared their knowledge and provided moral support) as well as expert advice in the form of faculty advisers. Lauren also was intrigued by Babson's Entrepreneurial Intensity Track (EIT), a second-year curriculum that was designed for students who were attempting to launch a business. Lauren enrolled, knowing she wanted to launch a business that would help children but unclear what that business might be.

Once she enrolled in Babson College and the EIT program, Lauren started thinking of ideas that might make a good business. Her ideas centered on her past experience; Lauren wanted to start a business that would help children. She thought about that plane trip and the unaccompanied child who seemed frightened. Could a plush toy business be a sustainable venture? The next section looks at a Quick Screen of Lauren's initial conception of FireFly Toys.

A Quick Screen of FireFly Toys

It became clear to Lauren very quickly that a focus only on children who traveled unaccompanied by adults was too small a niche to have the growth potential necessary to make a sustainable business. Therefore, Lauren broadened her vision to include children facing difficult life situations. Building on that premise, Lauren recognized that the key to helping children in distress was to facilitate communication between them and their adult caregivers. She broadened her concept to include not only plush toys (Comfort Creatures) but also

1. Story books about the Comfort Creature
2. Comfort Kits that included activities to use alongside or independently of the Comfort Creature
3. Probably most important, instructions for caregivers on how to use Comfort Creatures and Comfort Kits to communicate with children

Lauren originally intended to sell her products through traditional toy retailers but came to realize how hard it is to penetrate those channels. Thus, FireFly initially will sell its product through institutions (hospitals, philanthropic organizations) that work with children and then leverage those channels to gain access to specialty toy retailers. FireFly will outsource the manufacturing of the product.

As we look at the Quick Screen for FireFly Toys, remember that this is an initial investigation of whether the idea is an opportunity. When you complete the Quick Screen, you are giving best first assessments of the key criteria highlighted in the Quick Screen. You should be doing Quick Screens for multiple ideas; don't spend an inordinate amount of time trying to come up with precise estimates (e.g., how big the market is). Understanding how one idea stacks up relative to others will allow you to devote more time to refining your estimates and starting the business planning process. Clearly, every plan has its own flavor and objectives; however, this exercise should help you think about your own business planning process more clearly. To illustrate the dynamic nature of opportunities (see Exercise 2.1) we put ovals around Lauren's original assessment of certain criteria (market size and margins) and show how some changes to her original vision have improved the nature of the opportunity.

All new venture ideas rest on several critical assumptions that will make or break the business. As you view the FireFly Quick Screen, you'll note that the overall assessment is mixed. The toy industry is a notoriously difficult one to enter and succeed in. FireFly believes it can be successful by entering a growing educational toy niche and targeting therapeutic toys, a segment that may be emerging. For FireFly to be successful, it will have to secure distribution, which, as you will see as you progress through the book, it hopes to do by going directly to institutions (hospitals, schools, and philanthropic organizations) that cater to children's needs. If this strategy proves successful, FireFly is well positioned to thrive. If not, FireFly has to develop the specialty toy retailer channel, where competition for shelf space is much higher. The goal of the Quick Screen is to help you identify these critical assumptions before you spend time and effort on a more thorough business planning process. The Quick Screen raises questions that you should work to answer as you proceed through the business planning process. As you view FireFly's Quick Screen, what issues do you see? How would you advise Lauren to manage these issues?

Exercise 2.1 *Quick Screen: Firefly Toys*

I. Market- and Margin-Related Issues

Criterion	Higher Potential	Lower Potential	Comments
Need/want/ problem	Identified	Unfocused	Market needs tool to foster communication between caregivers and children coping with difficult life situations.
Customers	Reachable and receptive	Unreachable/ loyal to others	Parents and caregivers. Can reach through specialty toy stores and institutions that provide services to children, but it may be difficult to access these channels.
Payback to users	<1 year	>3 years	Immediate. Cost of toy is nominal compared to benefit.
Value added or created	IRR 40% +	IRR < 20%	Uncertain but expect parents to pay premium for product, which should result in higher returns
Market size	$50–100 million	<$10 million or +1 billion	Estimate therapeutic toy market ~$100M of $4B overall educational market.
Market growth rate	+20%	Less than 20%, contracting	Flat for toys overall, but some reports indicate educational toys are growing fast.
Gross margin	40%+ and durable	Less than 20% and fragile	Margins likely >50% but fragile depending on entrance of competitors.
Overall potential:			Niche has great promise, but overall toy market is tough.
1. Market	higher _____XXX___ avg	_____ lower	
2. Margins	higher _____XXX avg	_____ lower	

> The original focus on children flying unaccompanied is a small opportunity. As she broadened focus to children in distress, it became more attractive.

> Lauren's original vision of only selling a plush toy is fragile. It would be more difficult to maintain strong margins without the added value of the Caregiver's Guide or the Comfort Kit.

II. Competitive Advantages

	Higher Potential Lower Potential	Comments
Fixed and variable costs	Lowest >>> **XXX**>>>>>>>>> Highest	Mostly variable costs. Contract manufacturing minimizes fixed costs
Degree of control		
Prices and cost	Stronger >>>>>>>>>>> **XXX**> Weaker	High price elasticity, but may not be as bad in the therapeutic toy niche
Channels of supply and distribution	Stronger >>>>>>>>>>>> **XXX**> Weaker	Channels have strong power.
Barriers to entry	Strong >>>>>>>>>> **XXX**>>>> None	Low barriers at toy manufacturing level. All within channels.
Proprietary advantage	Stronger >>>>>>>>>>>>>> **XXX**> None	No dominant proprietary product.
Lead time advantage (product, technology, people, resources, location)	Stronger >>> **XXX**>>>>>>>>>>> None	No existing competitor has powerful brand or channel control yet within therapeutic toy space.
Service chain contractual advantage	Stronger >>>>>>>>>>> **XXX**> Weaker	No contractual advantage.
Contacts and networks	Stronger >>> **XXX**>>>>>>>>> Weaker	Founder has extensive background in child care but little background in toy industry.

Overall Potential						Comments
1. Costs	higher		**X**avg		lower	FireFly is entering the very competitive toy industry, but by going into a newly emerging therapeutic toy niche, there may be more potential. Specifically, prices and margins should be higher, and FireFly may have an early entrant edge.
2. Channel	higher		avg	**X**	lower	
3. Barriers to entry	higher		avg	**X**	lower	
4. Timing	higher	**X**	avg		lower	

(continues)

Exercise 2.1 *continued*

III. Value Creation and Realization Issues

	Higher Potential	Lower Potential	Comments
Profit after tax	10–15% or more and durable	<5%; fragile	Fragile. New entrants could cause price competition.
Time to breakeven	< 2 years	> 3 years	Requires that sales scale as expected.
Time to positive cash flow	< 2 years	> 3 years	Estimate 13 months.
ROI potential	40–70% +, durable	< 20%, fragile	Predict ~35% return on equity by year 5.
Value	High strategic value	Low strategic value	If successful with distribution and therapeutic toy segment grows as expected, potentially high acquisition value.
Capitalization requirements	Low–moderate; fundable	Very high; difficult to fund	~$700K required
Exit mechanism	IPO, acquisition	Undefined; illiquid investment	Possible acquisition, hope to grow the business.

Overall value creation potential				FireFly is an early
1. Timing	higher __**X**____avg_____ lower			mover in this niche. If it catches on, its
2. Profit/free cash flow	higher _____**X**_avg_____ lower			potential is great.
3. Exit/liquidity	higher _____avg__**X**____ lower			For instance, American Girl was acquired by Matel for $700M.

IV. Overall Potential

	Go	No Go	Go, If . . .	Comments
1. Margins and markets	X			Therapeutic market holds potential.

	Go	No Go	Go, If . . .	Comments
2. Competitive advantages			X	Early mover, bundled product, key is distribution.
3. Value creation and realization	X			Focus groups and limited sales suggest high value.
4. Fit: "O" + "R" + "T"			X	Will require angel financing, possibly adding team member with toy experience.
5. Risk-reward balance	X			Lauren's passion.
6. Timing	X			Good if market accessed now.

7. Other compelling issues: must know or likely to fail
   a. Distribution method must be fleshed out.
   b. Must have vision for additional products.
   c. Should find an evangelist in child care community.
   d. Should find a team member with specialty retail success.

Ideally, would-be entrepreneurs have several different concepts that they screen before deciding which one to pursue. More often than not, however, entrepreneurs already have a strong vision for an opportunity they are driven to pursue even if the obstacles are many. We applaud both types of entrepreneurs. In the latter scenario the Quick Screen will help you reshape the opportunity so that it is best positioned to succeed. There is no perfect deal. We find that entrepreneurs often ask, "What can go right?" whereas nonentrepreneurs ask, "What can go wrong?" The purpose of the business planning process is to identify "what can go right" and take steps to get there.

Readers' Assessment and Exercising Your Entrepreneurship Quotient (EQ)

Go back to the FireFly Quick Screen. An assessment of Lauren's Quick Screen exercises your EQ. How would *you* rate each criterion? We recommend that you use a colored pen to highlight your ranking versus ours. Do you see Lauren's prospects differently than she does? Why? Do you think her enhancements (adding the Comfort Kit and Caregivers Guide) improve the deal? For your own idea, make copies of the Quick Screen and have team members evaluate and rank criteria separately. These separate rankings create the foundation for a team meeting that allows each person to articulate his or her understanding of the opportunity. The result is a consolidated Quick Screen. Date that document and begin creating an opportunity audit trail.

Many readers will disagree with Lauren's assessment. Some will be critical and point out what can go wrong. Because there is no such thing as a perfect opportunity, the flaws are the easiest place to start. That's okay but not sufficient to move an opportunity forward. For each problem offer a solution; at least map the activities you'll need to do to move the assessment closer to the "go" position. For example, look at Quick Screen under "Market- and Margin-Related Issues." Make a list of ways to get Lauren's products into the hands of customers and move the assessment to the higher potential rating. How will your methods generate loyalty? Can her product or service be shaped in some way to create loyalty? Then go beyond the criticism and brainstorm about what might go *right*. How will good things move the Quick Screen evaluation and create value?

Venture Checkup and Thinking Big

A tenacious entrepreneur will shape his idea and move the Quick Screen ratings toward the "go" conclusion. But you have to remember that although the Quick Screen exercise is important, it is purely hypothetical until you take action. The questions the Quick Screen generates are its most important function. When you begin to take action, some of those questions will be answered and new questions will arise. Therefore, you will gain the skills needed to perform a venture checkup. Planning, action, and adjustments are integral to the entrepreneurial process. But before launch, the opportunity assessment and shaping process must answer the scope and scale question. Is Lauren thinking big enough?

Time and again the authors have observed the classic small business owner who, almost like a dairy farmer, is enslaved by and wedded to the business. Extremely long hours of 70, 80, or even 100 hours a week and rare vacations are often the rule rather than the exception. And these hardworking owners rarely build equity other than in the real estate they own for the business. The implication is clear: One of the big differences between the growth- and equity-minded entrepreneur and the traditional small business owner is that the entrepreneur thinks *bigger*. Longtime good friend Patricia Cloherty puts it this way: "It is critical to think big enough. If you want to start and build a company, you are going to end up exhausted. So you might as well think about creating a *big* company. At least you will end up exhausted and *rich*, not just exhausted!"

Pat has a wealth of experience as a venture capitalist and is past president of Patrioff & Company in New York City. She also served as the first female president of the National Venture Capital Association. In these capacities she has been a lead investor, board member, and creator of many highly successful high-technology and biotechnology ventures, many of which were acquired or achieved an initial public offering (IPO). The constant action and shaping activity inherent in new venture creation should be done in the context of thinking big. The "think big" process takes you on a journey, always treading the fine line between high ambitions and being totally out of your mind. How do you know whether the idea you are chasing is just another rainbow or has a pot of gold at the end? The truth is that you can never know which side of the line you are on—and can stay on—until you undertake the journey.

Once you are comfortable with the Quick Screen analysis, it is time to start thinking about the business plan. Before writing the different sections of the plan, it is useful to complete the Business Plan Guide.

The Business Plan Guide

The guide is based on the analytical framework described in the book and builds on the Quick Screen. The Business Plan Guide will allow you to draw on data and analysis developed in the opportunity screening exercises as you prepare the business plan.

As you proceed through the Business Plan Guide, remember that statements need to be supported with data whenever possible. Note that it is sometimes easier to present data in graphic, visual form. In fact, visual presentation often communicates your vision more effectively. Include the source of all data, the methods and/or assumptions used, and the credentials of the people doing research. If data on which a statement is based are available elsewhere in the plan, be sure to state where that information can be found.

Remember that the Business Plan Guide is just that—a guide. It is intended to be applicable to a wide range of product and service businesses. For any particular industry or market, certain critical issues are unique. In the chemical industry, for example, there are special issues of significance, such as increasingly strict regulations at all levels of government concerning the use of chemical products and the operation of processes, diminishing viability of the high capital cost, special-purpose chemical processing plants serving a narrow market, and long delivery times of processing equipment. In the electronics industry the special issues may be the future availability and price of new kinds of large-scale integrated circuits. Common sense should rule in applying the guide to your venture.

In Exercise 2.2 we illustrate how Lauren might complete this guide before she starts her business planning process. We have used broadly defined activities, as you probably would in your first cut. As you start completing the tasks, you'll identify subtasks that complement the major tasks outlined. Put these subtasks into the schedule as you identify them. Although we expect that your scheduling of key activities will change, the discipline of going through the process keeps you focused on what needs to be done. If you start slipping on the deliverable due dates, it may be a signal that you were too aggressive in scheduling your dates or may signal other problems. For example, if you see that one team member is consistently slow on the deliverable, that may indicate that she is not a good person to retain because she might let you down once the business is launched. Just as in the actual business plan, scheduling is a work in process. Revisit your schedule regularly.

Some Business Plan Basics: A Process

Writing a business plan takes time and effort. You can expect to spend 200 hours creating the first draft. That is time well spent not because it will ensure that you raise the necessary capital but because the process will help you answer the critical questions necessary to identify the opportunity and reshape it so that it becomes a better opportunity. Remember, business planning is a means to an end, not the end result. The

Exercise 2.2 *Business Plan Guide: Firefly Toys*

Name: Lauren McLaughlin
Venture: FireFly Toys
Date: May 2002

STEP 1 Segment Information into Key Sections

Establish priorities for each section, including individual responsibilities and due dates for drafts and the final version. When you segment your information, it is vital to keep in mind that the plan needs to be logically integrated and that information should be consistent. Note that since the market opportunity section is the heart and soul of the plan, it may be the most difficult section to write; however, it is best to assign it a high priority and begin working there first. Remember to include tasks such as printing in the list.

Section or Task	Priority	Person(s) Responsible	Date to Begin	First Draft Due Date	Date Completed or Final Version Due Date
Toy industry information	High	Megan	Immediately	June 8	July 27
Child psychiatry information	High	Lauren	Immediately	June 8	July 27
Identify competitive products	High	Megan	Immediately	June 8	July 27
Focus group with parents	High	Lauren	June 15	June 22	July 27
Focus group with child psychiatrists	High	Lauren	June 20	June 27	July 27
Learn about manufacturing overseas	Low	Megan	July 1	July 8	July 27
Explore toy store distribution channel	Medium	Megan	July 1	July 8	July 27
Case study on American Girl	Low	Lauren	As time permits	July 15	July 27

STEP 2 List Tasks That Need to Be Completed

Devise an overall schedule for preparing the plan by assigning priority, persons responsible, and due dates to each task necessary to complete the plan. It is helpful to break larger items (field work to gather customer and competitor intelligence, trade show visits, etc.) into small, more manageable components (such as phone calls required before a trip can be taken) and to include the components as tasks. *Be as specific as possible.*

(continues)

Exercise 2.2 *continued*

Task	Priority	Person(s) Responsible	Date to Begin	Date of Completion
Industry	High	Megan	June 15	June 30
Customer	High	Lauren	June 30	July 15
Competition	High	Megan	June 15	June 30
Company	Medium	Lauren	July 30	August 15
Product	High	Lauren	June 15	June 30
Marketing	High	Megan	June 30	July 15
Operations	Medium	Megan	August 1	August 15
Development	Medium	Megan	August 1	August 15
Team	Medium	Lauren	August 7	August 21
Critical risks	Low	Both	August 15	August 30
Offering	Low	Lauren	August 15	August 30
Financial plan	Medium	Lauren	Ongoing	August 15
Appendices	Low	Both	As needed	August 30

STEP 3 Combine the List of Segments and the List of Tasks to Create a Calendar

In combining your lists, consider if anything has been omitted and whether you have been realistic in what people can do, when they can do it, what needs to be done, and so forth. To create your calendar, place an X in the week when the task is to be started and an X in the week when it is to be completed and then connect the X's. When you have placed all tasks on the calendar, look carefully for conflicts or lack of realism. In particular, evaluate if team members are overscheduled.

Task	Week 1	2	3	4	5	6	7	8	9	10	11	12	13	14	15
Toy industry information	X—X														
Child psychiatry information	X—X														
Identify competitive products	X—X														
Focus group with parents			X—X												
Industry			X———X												
Competition			X———X												
Product			X———X												
Focus group with child psychiatrists				X—X											
Learn about manufacturing overseas				X—X											
Explore toy store distribution channel				X—X											

Task										Week					
	1	2	3	4	5	6	7	8	9	10	11	12	13	14	15
Customer					X	X									
Marketing					X	X									
Case study on American Girl						X	X								
Company								X	X						
Operations								X	X						
Development								X	X						
Team									X		X				
Critical risks										X		X			
Offering										X		X			
Financial plan												X		X	
Appendixes												X		X	

STEP 4 A Framework to Develop and Write a Business Plan

While preparing your plan you most likely will want to consider sections in an order different from the one presented in this book. Also, when you integrate your sections into the final plan, you may choose to present material somewhat differently. The key is to make it *your* plan.

actual document will be obsolete the moment it comes out of the printer. Like all battle plans, it needs modification once the shooting starts.

There is a common misperception that a business plan is used primarily for raising capital. Although a good business plan assists in raising capital, the primary purpose of the process is to help entrepreneurs gain a deep understanding of the opportunity they are envisioning. A business plan tests the feasibility of an idea. It is a dynamic process, comparable to solving a jigsaw puzzle. Once you start filling in the blanks, you start seeing the real picture. Is it truly an opportunity? Many would-be entrepreneurs doggedly pursue ideas that are not opportunities, and the time invested in a business plan would save thousands of dollars and hours spent on wild goose chases. For example, if a person makes $100,000 per year, spending 200 hours on a business plan equates to a $10,000 investment in time spent ($50 an hour times 200 hours). However, launching a flawed business concept can accelerate into millions in losses. Most entrepreneurial ventures raise enough money to survive two years even if the business ultimately will fail. Assuming that the only expense is the time of the lead entrepreneur, a two-year investment equates to $200,000, not to mention the lost opportunity cost and the likelihood that other employees were hired and paid and that other expenses were incurred. Do yourself a favor and spend the time and money up front in planning.

The business plan process not only can prevent an entrepreneur from pursuing a bad opportunity, it also can help entrepreneurs reshape their original visions into better opportunities. The business plan process involves raising a number of critical questions and then seeking answers to those questions. Part of that process involves talking to target customers and gauging their "pain." Those conversations with customers, as well as other trusted advisers, can assist you in better targeting the features and needs that customers most want. This pre-start-up work saves effort and money that an entrepreneur might spend trying to reshape the product after the launch has occurred. This is not to say that new ventures don't adjust their offerings on the basis of customer feedback, but the business plan process can anticipate some of those adjustments before the initial launch.

Perhaps the greatest benefit of this process is that it allows an entrepreneur to articulate the business opportunity to stakeholders in the most effective manner. The plan provides the background that allows an entrepreneur to communicate the upside potential and attract equity investment. The business plan provides the validation needed to persuade potential employees to leave their current jobs for the uncertain future of a new venture. It is also the instrument that can secure a strategic partner, key customer, or key supplier. In short, the business plan provides an entrepreneur the deep understanding he needs to answer the critical questions stakeholders will ask even if the stakeholders don't actually read the written plan. Completing a well-founded business plan gives an entrepreneur credibility in the eyes of various stakeholders. The process can sharpen thinking and strategies that define the risk and reward and ultimately the odds for success. In this book we will illustrate the most common type of business plan, but keep in mind that there are different types of business plans suitable for different purposes.

Types of Plans

A business plan can take a number of forms, depending on its purpose. The primary difference between business plan types involves length and detail. If outside capital is needed, a business plan geared toward equity investors or debt providers typically is 25 to 40 pages long. This type of plan is also a good primer for new employees or if you need to communicate the value of your enterprise to various stakeholders, such as a new supplier or customer. Entrepreneurs need to recognize that these stakeholders, especially professional equity investors such as venture capitalists and professional debt providers, will not read the entire plan. Thus, the entrepreneur needs to produce the plan in a format that facilitates spot reading. We will investigate the major sections that constitute business plans throughout this book. Our general rule of thumb is that less is more. For instance, we've seen a number of plans receive venture funding that were closer to 25 pages than to 40 pages.

A second type of plan—the operational plan—is primarily for the entrepreneur and her team to guide the development, launch, and initial growth of the venture. There is no length specification for this type of plan; however, having over 80 pages is common. The basic organization format for the two types of plans is the same; however, the level of detail tends to be much greater in an operational plan. This is where the entrepreneur gains the deep understanding so important in discerning how to build and run the business.

The last type of plan is called a dehydrated business plan. These plans are considerably shorter than the previous two, typically no more than 10 pages. Their purpose is to provide an initial conception of the business, a more concise articulation of the people, the opportunity, and the finances required. Therefore, it can be used to test initial reaction to the entrepreneur's idea. It is a document that the entrepreneur can share with her confidants and receive feedback before investing significant time and effort in a longer business plan. This book will illustrate the more traditional plan that can be used to raise capital and inform other stakeholders.

What type of plan will you write? Our guess is that you will use all three types. In our experience a dehydrated plan is good as an initial cut at what the business is. If you are working with a team, a dehydrated plan can be a road map to ensure that everyone has the same vision. Then you can delegate the writing of different portions of the plan to other team members. For instance, one person may write the marketing plan, and another may write the development plan. Since each team member has the dehydrated plan as a guide, this type will require less reconciliation when the entire plan is put together. We also find that dehydrated plans are good for sending to stakeholders before meeting with them. Investors are unlikely to read a 40-page plan unless they are really interested in the concept. Therefore, after you have completed the entire business planning process, come back and write a spiffy dehydrated plan for external consumption. The dehydrated plan can be a tool to build interest from investors, customers, and suppliers.

The operational business plan is really a compilation of all the intelligence you and your team have gathered on the opportunity. It goes into a fine-grained level of detail on not only the opportunity but also the steps you'll take in launching the business. It has too much detail for external stakeholders but is invaluable to you.

With that in mind, the remainder of this book will guide you through the business planning process. Keep in mind that although the chapters present the plan sections sequentially, the process is iterative. You'll write pieces of one section and then move to another section before coming back and completing other parts of the plan. We cannot stress enough that the business planning process is dynamic and that the end result, a written plan, is obsolete the moment it comes off the printer. The business plan is a living document, one that you should revisit and revise often. Enjoy the process.

3 GETTING STARTED

Perhaps the hardest part of writing a business plan is getting started. Compiling the data, shaping the data into an articulate story, and producing the finished product can be a daunting task. Thus, the best way to write a business plan is in steps. First, write a 25-word statement of your current vision. This provides a road map for you and others to follow as you start the planning process. Once the team agrees on the vision, expand it into a short expanded summary of five to six pages. This expanded summary provides details and gives you momentum as you start attacking major sections of the plan. Although all the sections interact and influence all the other sections, it is often easiest to write the product or service description first. This is usually the most concrete component of the entrepreneur's vision. Keep in mind, however, that writing a business plan isn't purely a sequential process. You will be filling in different parts of the plan simultaneously or in whatever order makes the most sense to you. Finally, after you have completed a first draft of all the major sections, it is time to go back and write a shorter, more concise executive summary (one to two pages). Not surprisingly, the executive summary will be quite different from the original summary because of all the learning and reshaping that the business plan process facilitates.

Perhaps the most important thing to consider as you begin this task is that the business plan is a living document. Although the first draft will be polished, most business plans are obsolete the day they come out of the printer. Entrepreneurs continuously update and revise their business plans since the entire context is changing constantly. Can anyone tell you who *all* your competitors are today, let alone in a month? Again, the important part of the business plan isn't the final product but the learning gleaned from going through the process. Through each iteration, you will learn more; for example, you will identify more competitors in the next iteration than in the first. The business plan is the novel of your vision. It articulates what you see in your mind as well as crystallizing that vision for you and your team. It also provides a history, a photo album, if you will, of the birth, growth, and maturity of your business. Each major revision should be kept and filed and occasionally looked back on for the lessons you have learned. We find writing a business plan exciting and creative, especially if one is working on it with a founding team. Whether it is over a glass of wine, beer, or coffee, talking about your business concept with your founding team is invigorating, and the business plan is a critical outcome of those discussions. Let us examine how to develop and write effective business plans.

The Story Model: A Plan for Whom?

One of the major goals for business plans is to attract and convince various stakeholders of the potential of your business. Therefore, you have to keep in mind how those stakeholders will interpret the plan: Who is the plan for—you, potential team members, a brain trust adviser, investors, customers? The guiding principal is that you are writing a story. All good stories have a plot line, a unifying thread that ties the characters and events together. The most successful businesses in America all have well-publicized plot lines, or, more appropriately, taglines. When you hear taglines, you immediately connect them to the business. For example, on hearing "absolutely, positively has to be there overnight," most people connect that tagline to Federal Express and package delivery. Similarly, "Just do it" is intricately linked to Nike and the image of athletic excellence (Exhibit 3.1). A tagline is a sentence or even a fragment of a sentence that summarizes the essence of your business. It is the plot line that every sentence, paragraph, page, and diagram in the business plan should correlate to. A useful tip that we share with every entrepreneur we work with is to put that tagline in a footer that runs on the bottom of every page. Most word-processing packages, such as Microsoft Word,

Exhibit 3.1 *Taglines*

Nike	*Just do it!*
Federal Express	*Absolutely, positively has to be there overnight*
McDonalds	*We love to see you smile*
Cisco Systems	*Discover all that's possible on the Internet*
Microsoft	*Where do you want to go today?*

enable you to insert a footer that you can see as you type. As you are writing, if the section doesn't build on, explain, or directly relate to the tagline, it most likely isn't a necessary component of the business plan. Rigorous adherence to the tagline facilitates writing a concise business plan.

The key to the story model is capturing the reader's attention. The tagline is the foundation, but in writing the plan you want to create a number of visual catch points. Too many business plans are text-laden, dense manifestos. Only the most diligent reader will wade through all that text to find the valuable nuggets. Help the reader by highlighting different key points throughout the plan. How do you create these catch points? Some effective techniques include extensive use of headings and subheadings, strategically placed bullet point lists, diagrams, charts, and sidebars.[1] The point is to make the document not only content-rich but visually attractive.

Now let's look at the major sections of the plan (Exhibit 3.2). Keep in mind that although there are variations, most plans have these components. It is important to keep your plan as close to this format as possible because many stakeholders are used to the format and it facilitates spot reading. If you are seeking venture capital, for instance, you want to facilitate quick perusal because it has been found that venture capitalists often spend as little as five minutes on a plan before rejecting it or putting it aside for further attention. If a venture capitalist (VC) becomes frustrated with an unfamiliar format, it is more likely that she will

---

[1]A running sidebar is a visual device positioned down the right-hand side of the page that periodically highlights some of the key points in the plan. Don't overload the sidebar, but one or two items per page can draw attention to highlights that maintain reader interest.

Exhibit 3.2 *Business Plan Outline*

I.	Cover
II.	Title Page
III.	Executive Summary
IV.	Industry, Customer, and Competitor Analysis
V.	Company and Product Description
VI.	Marketing Plan
VII.	Operations Plan
VIII.	Development Plan
IX.	Team
X.	Critical Risks
XI.	Offering
XII.	Financial Plan
XIII.	Appendixes

reject it rather than try to pull out the pertinent information. Although other types of investors, such as friends, family, and angels, may be more patient than a VC, keeping the VC reader in mind will help you write a concise, effective plan that is more likely to impress all stakeholders.

Cover Page

The cover of the plan should include the following information: company name, tagline, contact person and address, phone, fax, e-mail, date, disclaimer, and copy number. Most of this information is self-explanatory, but a few things should be pointed out. First, the contact person for a new venture should be the president or another founding team member. We have seen some business plans that failed to have the contact person's name and phone number on the cover. Imagine the frustration of an excited potential investor who can't find out how to contact the entrepreneur to get more information. More often than not, that plan will end up in the rejected pile. Second, business plans should have a disclaimer along these lines:

This business plan has been submitted on a confidential basis solely to selected, highly qualified investors. The recipient should not reproduce this plan or distribute it to others without permission. Please return this copy if you do not wish to invest in the company.

Controlling distribution is particularly important when you are seeking investment, especially if you do not want to violate Regulation D of the Securities Exchange Commission (SEC), which specifies how many unaccredited investors can invest in your firm.[2]

The cover also should have a line stating the copy number. For example, you often see on the bottom right portion of the cover a line that says "Copy 1 of 5 copies." Entrepreneurs should keep a log of who has copies so that they can prevent unexpected distribution. Finally, the cover should be eye-catching. If you have a product or prototype, a picture of it can draw the reader in. Similarly a catchy tagline draws attention and encourages the reader to look further. Let's take a look at the FireFly Toys cover page.

---

[2]Going into detail on SEC regulations is beyond the scope of this book; if in doubt, check with your lawyer. However, here are a few of the basics. If your total financing need (private placement) is under $1 million, there aren't any federal restrictions other than antifraud rules. If it is over $1 million, you can have only 35 unaccredited investors. The rest need to be accredited, which is defined as having a net worth greater than $1 million or an annual income over $200,000.

FireFly Cover Page

FireFly Toys, Inc.   "Creating Serious Play"

Note the company name
and tagline in the header.

Picture of company logo
attracts the eye. Nice visual.
Lauren might consider expanding
the logo to fill more of the page
and possibly eliminating the
written title.

FireFly Toys, Inc.

Contact person and
information are easy to find.

Lauren C. McLaughlin

549 Riverside Dr. #6B

New York, NY 10027

Lauren@fireflytoys.com

Business plan date allows
you to track version easily.
Remember, you probably will
have multiple versions of your
plan.

Dated: September 19, 2002
Copy 5 of 5

Control number and
disclaimer help you track who
has copies of the business plan.

Table of Contents

Continuing the theme of making the document easy to read, a detailed table of contents is critical. Many investors, for example, prefer to spot read business plans rather than reading them from front to back. Help those readers find the information they want. The table of contents should include major sections, subsections, exhibits, and appendices. The table gives the reader a road map to your plan. Note that the table of contents is customized to the specific business so that it doesn't correlate perfectly with the business plan outline in Exhibit 3.2. Nonetheless, a look at the FireFly plan shows that it includes most of the elements highlighted in the exhibit and that the order of information is basically the same.

The executive summary is always the first item in a business plan. The next three sections relate directly to the due diligence prescribed in the Timmons Model. The "Market Analysis" and "Competition" sections translate the opportunity analysis described in Chapter 1. "The Company" description is the unique way in which you will mine that opportunity. The "Team" section often comes later in the plan to provide an exclamation point. Until that point you have identified the opportunity, your company's solution, and how you will execute the plan. The team section shows that you have the horsepower to succeed.

FireFly Table of Contents

FireFly Toys, Inc. "Creating Serious Play"

> Major headings are designated as 1.0, 2.0, etc.. Subsections are designated as 2.1, 2.2, etc. This helps the reader navigate the table of contents and the plan itself.

TABLE OF CONTENTS

Executive Summary

This section is the most important part of the business plan. If you don't capture the readers' attention in the executive summary, it is unlikely that they will read any other parts of the plan. Therefore, you want to hit them with the most compelling aspects of your business opportunity right up front. *Hook the reader.* That means having the first sentence or paragraph highlight the potential of the opportunity. We have read too many plans that start with "Company XYZ, incorporated in the state of Delaware, will develop and sell widgets." Ho-hum. That doesn't excite us, but suppose the first sentence states: "The current market for widgets is $50 million, growing at an annual rate of 20%. Moreover, the emergence of the Internet is likely to accelerate this market's growth. Company XYZ is positioned to capture this wave with its proprietary technology, the secret formula VOOM. The founding team has over 60 years of experience in starting and building three companies in a related technology and market area. Two of these businesses were sold, and the third is a public company with sales over $100 million." This creates the right tone. It tells us that the potential opportunity is huge and that Company XYZ has a competitive advantage that enables it to become a big player in this market. Moreover, the strength of the founding team and its track record would be attractive to investors. We don't really care at this point that the business is incorporated or that it is a Delaware corporation (aren't they all?).

Common subsections within the executive summary include: description of opportunity, business concept, industry overview, target market, competitive advantage, business model and compelling economics, team, and offering. Remember that since this is an executive summary, all these components are covered in the body of the plan. We will explore them in detail in the remainder of the book.

Because the executive summary is the most important part of the finished plan, it should be written after you have gained deep learning by going through all the other sections.[3] The summary should be one to three pages, although we prefer that executive summaries be no more than two pages.

---

[3]Don't confuse the executive summary included in the plan with the expanded executive summary that we suggested you write as the first step in the business plan process. The two summaries are likely to be significantly different as the later summary incorporates all the deep learning you have gained throughout the process.

FireFly Executive Summary

1.0 EXECUTIVE SUMMARY

Use of headings facilitates spot reading.

Introduction:

Concisely lays out what the business is.

FireFly Toys is a therapeutic toy company dedicated to creating toys for children who are coping with a difficult life challenge or crisis. Examples of challenges or crises include bullying, nightmares, divorce, and illness. Whatever the cause, children are faced with many stressful challenges that can affect a child's psychological development and esteem, possibly leading to behavioral issues. Firefly has developed a unique line of therapeutic toys that enable caregivers and parents to:

These bullets highlight FireFly's customer value proposition.

1. Effectively communicate with children during difficult times
2. Provide children with comfort
3. Have fun

The Opportunity:

This is the hook. These trends suggest that the FireFly concept may have potential.

The opportunity derives from several converging trends:

Use of bullet points and bold help draw the reader's attention to the competitive advantage.

• **One in six children in the United States is coping with a crisis.**
 In any given year, nearly 72 million children under the age of 18 are coping with a personal crisis.[1]

This bullet shows that a large number of children are affected by the problem FireFly hopes to address. Also note that Lauren has footnoted the source of this statistic. Footnotes add credibility if they are from a respected source.

• **Therapeutic toys help children work through issues.**
 Child psychologists recognize the value of play therapy in helping children communicate and work through issues.

This bullet asserts that toys could be effective in dealing with this problem.

• **Child caregiver professionals are seeking more tools.**
 FireFly has attended several conventions of child care professionals, and attendees have validated our belief that new, specially designed toys can help children through these crises.

This bullet implies that the FireFly concept is valid.

---

[1] American Academy of Child and Adolescent Psychiatry, "A Call to Action: Children Need Our Help!" http://www.aacap.org/training/action_mc.pdf.

Business Concept:

FireFly has developed a specially designed bundled product line that provides the tools parents and caregivers need to communicate with a child in distress.

> Pictures of the product have impact and communicate that the company is making progress.

- **The Comfort Creature** is a tactile plush fleece doll designed with special features that help children communicate their feelings. The Comfort Creature comes with a story book showing the Comfort Creature managing a life crisis (e.g., a death in the family).

- **The Comfort Kit**, intended to be sold separately, is a specially designed backpack filled with toys, crafts, games, and additional story books featuring the Comfort Creature. The activities in the Comfort Kits are designed to help the child and caregiver connect and deal with a life crisis. To that end, a caregiver's guide instructs parents/caregivers on how to use the Comfort Creature, Comfort Kits, and story books to help the child deal with the situation. In addition, the company is upgrading its website to provide more resources for caregivers.

Parents and caregivers confirm that FireFly is a useful tool.

> *"My child wasn't willing to consider sleeping alone since her father died, but since we introduced Jordo she has slept by herself for a whole two weeks."*

> Quotes have impact. Testimonials validate company concept.

> *"Jordo sleeps at the end of my bed at night and protects me."*
>   Child, age 5

Industry Overview:

The international toy industry surpassed $55 billion[2] in sales in 2000. The U.S. traditional toy market was $25 billion in 2001 growing at approximately 2% per year.[3] The traditional toy market is led by Matel, Hasbro, and Lego, which account for 42% of all revenue.[4] However, certain niches provide opportunity for innovative companies.

> Concisely sizes overall market and growth rate.

> Gives sense of market structure: consolidated. This would suggest that the opportunity isn't that attractive within mainstream market.

---

[2]Diane Lee, "Toys and Games," Trade and Consumer Team, Hoovers On-line. 2001.
[3]*American Demographics*, 24(9): 14. October 2002.
[4]Mattel, Inc., Research Brief, Banc of America Securities, January 2003.

Gomez Advisors has found that educational toys are the fastest-growing segment of the toy industry, having reached $4 billion in 2000.[5] The gross margins in this segment tend to be 30 to 40% and are easier to maintain than the gross margins in the mass-market segment because there is a greater focus on specific target customers and distribution channels.

> FireFly is suggesting that the educational niche has more promise.

Target Market:

> FireFly suggests that there is a new segment within the education toy niche.

Within the educational toy market, there is an emerging therapeutic toy segment. There are two core customers: parents and professional caregivers. FireFly focuses on those **parents** who are aware that their child needs extra support during difficult life situations. Of the more than 32 million parents with young children, Simmons 1999 database suggests that nearly 2 million of them encountered a difficult life situation (such as moving or divorcing) and purchased a plush or educational toy.[6]

> Strategic use of bold font draws attention. FireFly is identifying one of its core customers.

> Suggests that parents are motivated to buy a product that helps the child.

Caregivers include nurses, preschool teachers, child psychologists, and child counselors. They work with children in settings where life challenges emerge as both crisis situations and regular developmental difficulties. Of the nearly 10 million such caregivers, more than 25% purchased a plush or educational toy in 1999.[7]

> Again, suggests that second core customer is also motivated to buy.

To reach these customers, FireFly will distribute its products through institutions where caregivers work and parents interact with the caregivers (philanthropic organizations, hospitals, and schools) with secondary distribution through specialty toy retailers and direct sales through FireFly's website and phones. This strategy provides FireFly an edge as few other toy companies sell to institutions.

> This is possibly one of FireFly's competitive advantages, assuming that it can get access to the institutions.

Competitive Advantage:

> Notice that FireFly's expected competitive advantage is bundled. It includes multiple elements.

FireFly's competitive advantage is summarized in the four points below:

1. A product that helps children **gain relief** from the crises they are facing.

2. An **affordable, simple solution** even an inexperienced caregiver can use to communicate effectively with a child going through a difficult life challenge.

3. **A creative way to communicate** with children at their own level in their own time.

---

[5]John Grossman, "Educational Retailer Learns Hard Lesson." *Inc.*, April 2000, Vol. 22, Issue 5.
[6]Simmons Choices 3: [1999] Simmons Market Research Copyright [1999]. Simmons Market Research. All rights reserved.
[7]Ibid.

4. **An integrated system** of products that includes both comforting toys for the child and important advice for the caregiver. The products and advice specifically address the different educational and therapeutic challenges both the caregiver and the children are facing.

Management:

Lauren Creamer McLaughlin, founder and CEO, has 10 years of experience working with children in crisis. Megan MacDonald, director of marketing, has 6 years of marketing experience, including an internship at Hasbro, Inc. Both graduated from the F.W. Olin Graduate School of Business at Babson College.

> This section is too concise. Tell us each management team member's role, involvement, investment, and ownership.

FireFly has assembled an advisory board that is expert in child development, including Julie Reiss, PhD Developmental Child Psychology, Vassar College; Richard Cook, Executive Director of Winston child care center and faculty member of Boston City University; and Lisa Andrews, Head Preschool Teacher at Winston child care center.

> The advisers seem to be a strength. Emphasize that by giving more detail on their skills and what they offer the company.

Financial Highlights:

> A brief overview of your expectations gives investors a sense of the potential return.

FireFly expects to enjoy attractive gross margins due to our premium pricing and low-cost production. The table below highlights our expected performance.

	2003	2004	2005	2006	2007
REVENUES	787,030	4,367,320	8,806,940	15,274,640	24,244,345
COST OF REVENUE	367,949	1,295,373	2,368,554	4,159,758	6,447,854
GROSS PROFIT	419,081	3,071,947	6,438,387	11,114,883	17,796,491
% of Revenues	53%	70%	73%	73%	73%
Total Operating Expenses	619,079	1,918,737	3,455,839	5,718,438	10,211,094
Net Earnings before Taxes	(199,999)	1,135,210	2,982,547	5,396,444	7,595,397

Status and Offering:

> The snapshot suggests aggressive but doable revenue assumptions and very high gross margins (make sure the plan supports this assertion). The economics appear attractive.

FireFly has raised $55,000 to date, using those funds to produce 500 Jordos (Comfort Creature) and 500 Comfort Kits, including all ancillary materials (books, caregiver guide, etc.). The company has sold 126 Jordos and 75 Comfort Kits. FireFly is seeking $320,000 in angel funding in order to produce 25,000 more product, create and introduce a second product line, and build out the infrastructure to achieve these goals.

> It is a good idea to communicate what you have accomplished already. It portrays an action orientation and suggests that you can execute your strategy.

Summary

The most important part of any business plan is the executive summary. Although you should write the final version that is included in the business plan after all the other sections have been completed, drafting an extended version before digging into the other sections can help you clarify your vision. You can share this early draft with fellow team members to ensure that you are all on the same page. The final version of the executive summary is the most important part of the plan. It not only acts as a hook to entice investors and other stakeholders to take a closer look, it is also your concise articulation of the opportunity. We find that entrepreneurs who can articulate their opportunity clearly are more successful in persuading others to join or invest. The remaining chapters examine in detail the different sections of the plan.

4 INDUSTRY: ZOOM LENS ON OPPORTUNITY

The goal of this section is to illustrate the opportunity and show why there is a significant market to capture. Exhibit 4.1 shows the typical structure for this section. We start with the industry definition. What is the broader industry in which your venture will participate? We try to be expansive about the industry definition to make the vastness of the opportunity clear even if we will attack a specific niche. For instance, FireFly operates in the toy industry. We can use the opportunity component from the Timmons Model described in Chapter 1 to articulate the opportunity. Detail the industry size, the growth rate, and the major players. Talk about the nature of the industry. Is it emerging, consolidated, mature? Next, talk about the major trends occurring in the industry. For example, FireFly highlights several favorable trends. The educational toy segment, which FireFly suggests is the overall niche in which therapeutic toys falls, is growing faster than is the overall toy market. Explaining the pertinent trends bolsters the opportunity and suggests what white space there may be within the industry. Your assessment of industry trends is an important part of the articulation of your vision.

The next step is to define the segments within the industry. For example, FireFly segments toys by plush animals/dolls, video games, educational, activities and games, and the catchall "other." Then you need to define your niche in terms similar to those you used to define the industry. Specifically, detail the size, growth, major players, and trends that affect the environment in which you will enter.

Exhibit 4.1 *Industry Section*

I. **Industry definition**
   A. Size
   B. Growth
   C. Major players
   D. Trends
II. **Segments**
   A. Define
   B. Your segment
   C. Size, growth, major players
   D. Trends

A common error in writing this section is to focus on your own company. It's premature to talk about your company before setting the scene. Instead, use a dispassionate, arm's-length analysis of the industry with the goal of highlighting a space or gap that is underserved. You are creating the stage to introduce your company a bit later in the plan. Remember, most people will have read the executive summary, and so they know what your concept is and can use that to assess whether they believe your description of the competitive environment.

As the entrepreneur, you should keep in mind how people will read the plan. Every statement and statistic you cite adds credibility and reinforces your story, but it also triggers areas that readers will want to investigate. As we read plans, for instance, we think about ways to validate entrepreneur claims. In other words, we start constructing a due diligence schedule. That means identifying key assumptions such as whether the therapeutic niche has the potential that Lauren claims. To validate that, we might contact our brain trust members (people who have expertise in the industry and can gauge whether Lauren's scenario makes sense) and talk to customers, distributors, and even competitors. Note that the types of actions investors or other stakeholders might take mirror actions that you as an entrepreneur should have taken. Thus, entrepreneurs often can guide stakeholders in their due diligence by connecting them with customers and others with whom the entrepreneur has spoken. Let's take a look at the FireFly industry section.

FireFly Industry Analysis Section

2.0 MARKET ANALYSIS

2.1 Industry

In 2000, the international toy industry surpassed $55 billion[1] in sales. The U.S. traditional toy market was $25 billion in 2001, growing at approximately 2% per year.[2] Traditional toys include plush animals, dolls, games, and so forth (see Figure 2.1) but not video games. The toy industry is consolidated, with three major players, Hasbro Inc., Mattel, and Lego, accounting for 42% of the revenues.[3] Several trends impact the industry.

Sizes the market and growth rate.

Identifies industry structure and the fact that it is fairly consolidated. This would make the opportunity less attractive as these major players probably have more power in the distribution channels. Investors would keep this in mind as they read the rest of the plan to gauge how well the proposed strategy counters this weakness.

Less Time Available for Unstructured Play

Children are more scheduled today. On average, children 3 to 11 years of age spend 6 hours a day in school or preschool versus only 4 hours a day in the 1980s.[4] Outside of school, kids continue structured play with sports, dance, and other extracurricular activities. This all results in 30 minutes less per day of unstructured play than was the case in the 1980s.[5] Thus, children have less time for toys.

Identifies major trends and bolds them so that they capture the reader's attention.

This trend suggests that the educational niche is of growing importance.

Getting Older Younger Phenomenon

Kids face more pressure at an earlier age, whether it is a lack of downtime or an increased emphasis on scholastic performance. In 1999, 38% of children reported that they received rewards for getting good grades, up from 27% 2 years earlier.[6] This has led to a convergence of play and other elements in the child's life. Thus, toys connect these disparate elements of a child's life, such as education and play.

One of the tricky parts of building your story is gathering data that validate your claims. Lauren has pulled disparate statistics from numerous sources to build the segmentation diagram below. We couldn't find, for example, the segmentation statistics put together the way Lauren has. Many of the data we saw didn't list education toys as a separate segment. Instead, it appears that most data assumed educational toys could cut across categories, although that was never stated explicitly. You need to be careful that your data have integrity, but as we said in Chapter 1, if it is hard to find the data surrounding the opportunity, it may mean that it has potential.

Growth of Educational Toy Market

Internet research and analysis firm Gomez Advisors found that educational toys are the fastest-growing segment of the

---

[1]Diane Lee, "Toys and Games," Trade and Consumer Team, Hoovers On-line. 2001.
[2]*American Demographics*, 24(9): 14, October 2002.
[3]Mattel, Inc., Research Brief, Banc of America Securities, January 2003.
[4]J. Raymond, "Kids Just Want to Have Fun," *American Demographics*, 2002, 22(2): 57–65.
[5]Ibid.
[6]Ibid.

toy industry, having reached $4 billion in 2000.[7] Consumer purchasing trends indicate that parents want wholesome toys that remind them of their childhood and that provide their children with tools for learning. Educational toys usually are sold at smaller specialty retail stores or trusted toy catalogs where there is a greater emphasis on child development and a more high-touch sales process.

Figure 2.1 *Toy Industry $25B*

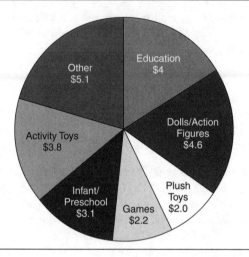

Seasonality

Seasonality continues to be a key factor in the toy industry, with 45% of all toy sales occurring during the fourth quarter. At the same time, however, toys are relatively immune to downturns in the economy. Brit Beemer, president of America's Research Group, found that "Parents may cut back on spending, but not on their kids."[8]

> This section goes from the industry overview down to the target niche. It is interesting to note that the therapeutic toy niche isn't defined by anyone else. Lauren is creating a story, saying a new niche is emerging. She is foreshadowing what will be one of her company's distinctive advantages. Note that this trend also links directly to FireFly's business model. It suggests revenue drivers and cost drivers (marketing distribution and so forth).

Therapeutic Toy Niche

Therapeutic toys are an emerging niche within the educational toy space. Therapeutic toys can be defined as toys that are used to help kids who are working through either a physical or a mental situation. Although many toys can be useful in such cases, therapeutic toys are specifically designed to help children in their recovery process. FireFly will focus primarily on children facing mental crises, such as death in the family or divorce.

---

[7]John Grossman, "Educational Retailer Learns Hard Lesson." *Inc.,* April 2000, Vol. 22, Issue 5.
[8]"Traditional Toys Make Comeback; Parents Seek Imaginative, Low-Cost Gifts," Hoovers On-line 2001

Therapeutic toys leverage trends in the overall market and counter others. For example, as play time decreases and goal-oriented toys become more common, therapeutic toys are a natural extension to the education niche.

> Note how this paragraph ties together the various identified trends and suggests how they naturally lead to the therapeutic space.

Therapeutic toys help parents connect with kids (goal orientation) in the limited time they have together each day (time available for unstructured play). Therapeutic toys also may be less sensitive to seasonality as they are more than just a gift; they are a tool to help children manage crisis (which can happen at any point in the year).

The potential market is large. According to the American Academy of Child and Adolescent Psychiatry,[9] one in six American children under the age of 18 is coping with a personal crisis in any given year. Therapeutic toys can help children overcome these crises.

> This helps size the therapeutic niche. It would have been better to take this further and give a raw number of how many children this means.

---

[9]American Academy of Child and Adolescent Psychiatry, "A Call to Action: Children Need Our Help!" http://www.aacap.org/training/action_mc.pdf.

Customer

Once the plan has defined the market space it plans to enter, the target customer has to be examined in detail. The entrepreneur needs to define who the customer is by using demographic and psychographic information. The better the entrepreneur can define her customer, the more apt she is to deliver a product the customer truly wants. A venture capitalist recently told one of the authors that the most impressive entrepreneur is the one who comes into his office and not only identifies who the customer is in terms of demographics and psychographics but also can name that customer by address, phone number, and e-mail address. When you understand who your customers are, you can assess what compels them to buy, how your company can sell to them (direct sales, retail, Internet, direct mail, etc.), how much it is going to cost to acquire and retain them, and so forth. A schedule inserted into the text that describes customers based on the basic parameters can be very powerful. It communicates a lot of data quickly.

The key to understanding your customers is to get to know them. The best means of doing so, prior to launch, is to talk to them. Many would-be entrepreneurs fail to talk to their customers. They assume since they would be interested in their own product, so would others. This is often a fatal assumption. We encourage you to have informal conversations with your customers. If at all possible, observe them doing the activity or work that your product or service would make better, easier, or more cost-effective. Taking such action will help you modify your offering so that you can better meet customer expectations. For example, the founder of FireFly, Lauren McLaughlin, has years of experience working with children, especially those who have faced emotional difficulties. She built on her personal experience working with distressed children by speaking with their parents. She learned that parents felt helpless in trying to comfort their children. The parents didn't really understand what was bothering their kids. It basically came down to a communication barrier, and Lauren knew from her professional experience that toys can bridge that barrier. She then talked to a number of child psychologists and other experts who worked with children to gain a deep understanding of what her customer wanted. Her next step was to do a limited run of the product and see if she could sell some Comfort Creatures. The fact that she has taken these steps and passed these milestones communicates her action orientation and lessens the perceived risk that the venture won't succeed.

Talking to your customer is invaluable, but you also can gain insight by talking to others who have knowledge of your customer. Talk to your potential suppliers, competition,[1] and other people and companies involved in the market space. Going to a trade show is invaluable. In such venues, people are there to share information, and so your competitors might be more apt to discuss what they perceive as the customers' needs. Lauren, for example, attended the American International Toy Fair in New York as well as trade shows for key customers such as the Play Therapy Association Conference. The key to understanding your customer is to do primary research. Get out there and interact with the customer.

In many cases, the end user is not the person who makes the purchase decision. For example, the end users of FireFly toys are children age 2 to 6. The person who buys the product is the parent, the caregiver, or possibly an institution that supports parents. Each of these players has

---

[1]In the age of fraud, as evidenced by Enron, WorldCom, Global Crossing, and Arthur Andersen, we can't stress enough the need to act in an ethical manner. When talking to competitors, never misrepresent yourself as a customer. Many of your competitors started out as entrepreneurs as well, and they understand the difficulties you are facing, and so often they will talk to you freely except in the most competitive, cutthroat industries.

a different motivation, and you as the entrepreneur need to be aware of that motivation so that you can design a product or service that meets their needs. For example, philanthropic organizations want to support children. In this case, Lauren needs to communicate how the product helps parents help their children. The child wants a lovable, interesting toy, and so FireFly also has to develop a toy that children will play with. Understanding how all these users, influencers, and actual buyers interact with each other will help you design the product or service that best meets their needs.

FireFly Customer Section

2.2 THE CUSTOMER

> This section describes the customer audiences FireFly speaks to.

FireFly's target end customers are caregivers who are meeting the needs of a preschool-aged child or children coping with a stressful life challenge. These caregivers are split into two segments:

> Identifies the buyer.

> Identifies the user.

> Careful attention to the decision maker(s).

- Parents and direct caregivers of preschool-aged children
- Caregivers in institutional settings.

Although many of these customers will buy the product directly, an important distribution player is philanthropic organizations and hospitals that will provide the products directly to the children as part of their treatment.

Parents and Direct Caregivers:

FireFly's target market segment is composed of literate adults between 25 and 49 years of age with annual incomes of $50,000 or more. This age range captures the bulk of parents, 59.5 million of the more than 75 million U.S. parents in 1999. Caregivers in this group purchase 67% of children's products and services. Parents buy toys for any number of reasons, including special occasions (birthdays, Christmas, etc.), requests from the child, and to achieve certain goals (child development[1]).

> Demographic description of customer. Lauren clearly believes that an educated middle- and upper-income parent is more likely to buy her product.

> Lauren needs to segment parents further. It is highly unlikely that a start-up can market to 80% of all parents, nor would it be effective to do so. Which subsegment is the sweet spot?

> Psychographic description.

FireFly focuses on those parents who are aware that their child needs extra support during difficult life situations. Of the more than

---

[1] Simmons Choices 3: [1999] Simmons Market Research Copyright [1999]. Simmons Market Research. All Rights Reserved.

32 million parents with young children, Simmons 1999 database suggests that nearly 2 million of them encountered a difficult life situation (such as moving or divorcing) and purchased a plush or educational toy. This suggests a strong market from parents whose children are facing tough life situations.[2]

> Using statistics validates that psychographic motivation compels the customer to buy. The question becomes how to you reach the 2 million primary target customers.

Caregivers in Institutions:

> Identifying the different professionals who would be interested suggests possible strategies on how to reach them, such as conferences and trade shows. We'll look at this again in the marketing section.

These caregivers include nurses, preschool teachers, child psychologists, and child counselors. They work with children in settings where life challenges emerge as both crisis situations and regular developmental difficulties. Of the nearly 10 million such caregivers, more than 25% purchased a plush or educational toy in 1999. They tend to purchase new products at conferences, through newsletter recommendations, or through the recommendation of another caregiver.[3]

Hospitals, Philanthropic Organizations and Schools:

> This suggests that institutions are influencers and may motivate the caregivers to buy.

> Recognizes that FireFly may get large sales through these organizations.

> The list shows that Lauren has done her homework. It also communicates that she has identified potential buyers and started to foster potential sales. If Lauren has moved beyond preliminary talks, letters showing support (included in the appendix) would provide strong validation of her business.

Many caregivers and parents receive advice on products from hospitals and organizations that focus on children's issues. These organizations also may act as the buyer and give the product to children through the caregivers. The list below includes some examples of potential institutional buyers. FireFly has talked with these organizations, and they have expressed interest in working with FireFly.

Hospitals
- Dana Farber Cancer Institute
- Tufts Medical Center

Philanthropic Organizations
- YWCA International
- YMCA
- UNICEF
- Save the Children
- Child Life Programs
- National Resource Center against Domestic Violence

---

[2]Ibid.
[3]ibid.

Schools
- The Lemberg Preschool at Brandeis University
- The Wimphfeimer Nursery School at Vassar College
- The Lab School at the University of Chicago

Competition

The competitive analysis is derived directly from the customer analysis. Specifically, you have identified your market segment and described what the customer looks like and wants. The key factor leading to the competitive analysis is what the customer wants in a particular product. These product attributes form a basis of comparison with your direct and indirect competitors. A competitive profile matrix is a useful tool to communicate those attributes and show how the competition is addressing them. The matrix figure not only creates a powerful visual catch point, it conveys information regarding gaps in the current offerings, setting the stage to describe your competitive advantage and the basis for your company's strategy. After a brief introductory paragraph, the competitive profile matrix should lead the section and be followed by text describing the analysis and its implications.

Creating a competitive profile matrix requires an understanding of what the marketplace values, the key success factors. In other words, what makes the customer buy one company's product over another's? Think about a restaurant. People often choose to dine in restaurants based on a number of factors, including the location, the price and quality of the food, and the atmosphere. Because you have a strong understanding of your customer, you should be able to identify the key success factors for your market space. Once you have the key success factors, you list your competition and your venture in the matrix and then evaluate how each company fares in dealing with the key success factors.

Finding information about your competition can be easy if a company is public, harder if it is private, and very difficult if it is operating in "stealth" mode (it hasn't yet announced itself to the world). Most libraries have access to databases that contain a mother lode of information about publicly traded companies (see Exhibit 4.2 for some sample sources), but privately held companies and stealth ventures represent a greater challenge. The best way for savvy entrepreneurs to gather this in-

Exhibit 4.2 *Sample Source for Database Information on Public/Private Companies*

Infotrac—Indexes/abstracts of journals, general business and finance magazines, market overviews, and profiles of public and private firms.

Factiva—Searchable index of articles from over 3,000 newspapers.

Lexis/Nexis—Searchable index of articles.

Dun's Principal International Business—International business directory

Dun's One Million Dollar Premium—Database of public and private firms with revenues greater than $1 million or more than eight employees.

Hoover's Online—Profiles of private and public firms with links to websites, etc.

Corp Tech—Profiles of high-technology firms.

Reuter's.com—Detailed financial information on 1.4 million international securities that can be manipulated in tables and graphs.

RDS Bizsuite—Linked databases providing data and full-text searching on firms.

Bloomberg—Detailed financial data and analyst reports.

formation is through their networks and at trade shows. Who should be in the entrepreneur's network? First and foremost are the customers the entrepreneur hopes to sell to in the near future. Just as you are (or should be) talking to your potential customers, your competition is interacting with customers every day and your customers probably are aware of the stealth competition that is on the horizon. Although many entrepreneurs are fearful (verging on the brink of paranoia) that valuable information will fall in the wrong hands and lead to new competition that invalidates the current venture, the reality is that entrepreneurs who operate in a vacuum (meaning they don't talk to customers or show up at trade shows, etc.) fail far more often than do those who talk to everybody they can. Talking allows entrepreneurs to get invaluable feedback that enables them to reshape the product offering before launching a product that may or may not be accepted by the marketplace. Network not only to find out about your competition but also to improve your own venture concept.

Once you have completed your competitor analysis, the stage is set to talk about your venture. That is the reason we suggest you include your venture in the matrix. It highlights where your venture expects to have a competitive advantage.

FireFly Competitor Section

> Typically, we would suggest that you provide an overview of the competition outside your niche (indirect competition) and also substitutes for your product as that may influence competition within your space. For example, it is plausible that other education toy companies will enter the therapeutic space. Thus, Lauren may want to discuss some of the larger players in the educational segment as a group before highlighting her closest competitors. There are also substitutes for toys that may help foster communication between parents and children, such as sessions with conselors.

3.0 COMPETITION

The therapeutic toy segment is emerging from the educational toy niche. Currently, there are few competitors in this space, but like the overall toy industry, the segment has the potential to be highly competitive with low barriers to entry and multiple niche players. The key to success is differentiating the product based on a number of attributes, including price, quality, branding, distribution, and ancillary features. Exhibit 3.1 highlights three of FireFly's primary competitors and shows how FireFly compares to them.

> Identifies the attributes on which companies compete within the therapeutic niche.

Exhibit 3.1 *The Competitive Matrix*

> The matrix summarizes the competitors and illustrates how FireFly compares.

Company	Folkmanis	Manhattan Toys	The Spinoza Company	FireFly
Product	Puppets	Toys, stuffed animals, puppets	Teddy bears and audiotapes	Comfort Creatures and Kits
Product price	$20–$100	$10–$100	$20–$240	$40–$65
Features	High-quality, handmade	Attractive materials/ designs, simple	Plush, cassette tape player inside, speakers	Bundled toys. Plush animals, books, kits, caregiver guide
Therapeutic	Possibly, but not focus	No	Yes	Yes
Caregiver information	No	No	Limited	Yes
Packaging	On the shelf, with a tag	Cardboard tags, can touch product	Plastic-shipped	On the shelf, with a tag
Marketing/ advertising	Website, puppet shows, in-store displays	Website, in-store displays	Website, mailings, local charity partnerships	Website, special events, PR, ads
Distribution	Specialty stores, e-tailers, catalogs	Independent, toy stores, hospitals, museums.	Website, phone orders	Hospitals, philanthropic organizations, phone orders, specialty stores
Sales	$2.2 million	$8.9 million	~$1 million	N/A

> This is a key feature that Lauren clearly believes will provide a competitive advantage.

> Clearly no dominant player

> Remember, a value-added investor is one who probably knows the toy industry. These points must ring true for them.

The highlighted competitors have high quality standards and strong distribution. The factors in the matrix were chosen because they are the primary areas of competition within the toy industry. Companies first compete on product quality; however, customers do differentiate based on price and brand. The greatest challenge and strength of any toy company lies in the distribution channels. These companies have become important players within the educational market because of their ability to integrate the above factors.

> The following summaries provide some texture about the competitors listed in the matrix.

Folkmanis:

Folkmanis is a premier family-owned puppet manufacturer founded 25 years ago. Folkmanis[1] markets a variety of puppets that have been used for therapeutic purposes. However, the company does not promote its puppets as therapeutic toys and is not expected to do so in the future. The puppets do not come with any ancillary support for caregivers.

Manhattan Toys:

Manhattan Toys is a private company established in 1979. They design an array of toys from plush dolls to developmental toys. Manhattan Toy's mission is to create toys that engage children and their parents in creative, meaningful play. They have deeply penetrated the specialty retail market; 9,000 specialty retailers carry their products. These specialty stores range from museum and hospital gift stores to fashionable clothing stores.[2] Manhattan is perhaps the strongest competitor in this field. However, its distribution channels favor a broad retail market. Additionally, their toys lack therapy specific features.

The Spinoza Company:

A communication specialist and a special education teacher founded the Spinoza Company in 1984. The core product of the company is the Spinoza Bear, a soft teddy bear designed to be a resource for parents and teachers. Inside the bear is a cassette player and speakers that play special audiotapes sold by the company. The purpose of the bear is to provide a comforting presence that delivers lighthearted messages. They sell 8,000 bears a year across the country and in Canada primarily through connections with hospitals, hospice programs, and charity organizations, which purchase the bears for children in need. The core product price is $99.95.[3] Spinoza's bears have therapeutic features that set them apart, but the bears are priced very high.

---

[1]www.folkmanis.com.
[2]www.manhattantoy.com.
[3]www.spinozabear.com.

Summary:

All these companies produce products that have the
potential for therapeutic use, but only Spinoza actively taps
that market. The keys for success, aside from quality, are
to build strong relationships within the hospital, philanthropic organization, and
school distribution channels.

> The summary highlights the
> key implications for success,
> namely, the importance of
> building strong distribution
> through nontraditional channels.

Chapter Summary

The industry, customer, and competition section of the plan lays the platform for you to introduce your vision. It is best to use a dispassionate
tone. You need to present quantitative data (footnoting the source) to
describe the industry, customer, and competitors. The more rigorously
you describe and validate the context in which your venture will compete, the better you will understand how to compete. In other words,
this portion of the business planning process is where you often gain the
deepest learning. This learning will help you make better decisions. Furthermore, presenting this information well will strengthen your story and
impress investors. Remember, when you build a house, everything rests
on the foundation. If that foundation is weak, the house will crumble.
This section of the plan is the foundation on which the other sections
build. Build it thoughtfully and completely.

5 COMPANY AND PRODUCT DESCRIPTION: SELLING YOUR VISION

Completing the dispassionate analysis described in Chapter 4 lays the foundation for describing your company and concept. This is the place to be passionate and sell your vision. Use both rational data and emotional appeals that support your story. Exhibit 5.1 lays out the major sections covered in this part of the plan. In the first paragraph identify the company's name, state where it is incorporated, and give a brief overview of the concept for the company. Be clear but succinct in describing the product or service in this introductory paragraph. In the following paragraphs you can go into greater detail. The first paragraph also should highlight what the company has achieved to date, the milestones you have accomplished that show progress. Investors and stakeholders view action-oriented entrepreneurs who have accomplished milestones much more favorably.

More space should be used to describe the product. Graphic representations can be powerful. Building from the competitive profile matrix in the previous section, highlight how your product fits into the customer value proposition. What is incorporated into your product, and what value add do you deliver to the customer? This section should identify your venture's competitive advantage clearly and forcefully. Based on

Exhibit 5.1 *Company and Product Description*

- Company description
- Product description
- Competitive advantage
- Entry strategy
- Growth strategy

your competitive analysis, why is your product better, cheaper, and/or faster than what customers currently have access to? Your advantage may be a function of proprietary technology, patents, distribution, and the like. In fact, the most powerful competitive advantages are derived from a bundle of factors because that makes them more difficult to copy. Fire-Fly claims its uniquely bundled product (Comfort Creature, Comfort Kit, story book, and caregiver manual) creates value for caregivers. In fact, Lauren believes that caregivers will pay a premium for her product. Fire-Fly is making a claim that its offering is "better" than what is out there. FireFly also is using unique distribution channels (hospitals, philanthropic organizations, and institutions) to reach customers. This, coupled with the better product, creates a stronger competitive advantage.

Once you have delineated your product, a perceptual map of the product and your competitors' products communicates what makes your company special. Pick two or three of the key attributes identified in the competitor profile matrix and show how your venture differs from the competition. A competitor perceptual map visually illustrates the gaps in the market you expect to fill. We suggest that you bullet point the other elements that form the basis of your product or service competitive advantage.

As you can see, the business plan leads the reader in a logical progression. The goal is to create an understanding of your vision and make it tangible. Again, we build from previous work, in this case our clear description of the product, to the strategy for introducing that product. Many business plans falter here. Crafting a finely honed wedge to insert a new venture into a marketplace is essential for success. Think about taking a long walk. If you start on the wrong road, the trip can be extended dramatically or you may never reach your destination. Therefore, the goal is to communicate how you enter the industry and survive for the first couple of years while you are building your customer base and refining your business model. Since most new ventures are resource-constrained, especially in terms of available capital, it is crucial that the lead entrepreneur establish the most effective way to enter the market. Based on the analysis in the market and customer sections, entrepreneurs need to identify the primary target audience (PTA). Focusing on a particular subset of the overall market niche allows new ventures to utilize scarce resources effectively to reach those customers and prove the viability of the concept.

FireFly has started executing its entry strategy. It has outsourced production of the product and completed an initial production run. It has been experimenting with different distribution channels that might best reach its PTA. Lauren appears to be leaning toward professional caregivers who will use the product in their work with children and let the children take it home with them. To complete a successful entry, FireFly will need to develop one of the channels fully, say, through a philanthropic organization such as the YMCA. Moving product through that channel will help FireFly improve its production model by running larger batches and managing shipping better. However, using only one channel in the FireFly case probably would limit the upside potential. Lauren needs to have a vision for growth.

The business plan also should sell the entrepreneur's vision for growth because that indicates the true potential for the business. Investors in particular need to assess the growth potential because that is what drives their returns. As part of the storytelling you need to lay out the strategy and resultant scenario that you believe is most likely. Thus, a paragraph or two should be devoted to the firm's growth strategy. If the venture achieves success in its entry strategy, it will generate internal cash flow that can be used to fuel the growth strategy or be attractive enough to get further equity financing at improved valuations. The growth strategy should talk about the secondary target audience and the tertiary target audiences the firm will pursue. FireFly's growth will be driven by entering other distribution channels, especially specialty toy stores. If FireFly is successful in its entry strategy, it will build some recognition that Lauren can use to persuade specialty toy stores to carry her products. Thinking ahead to the next section of the business plan, the marketing section of the business plan must support your entry and growth strategies.

FireFly Company Section

4.0 THE COMPANY: FIREFLY TOYS

Headquartered in New York City, FireFly is a therapeutic toy company

> Identifies what the company does and gives a sense of its mission.

dedicated to creating toys for children who are coping with a difficult life challenge or crisis. Examples of challenges or crises include bullying, nightmares, divorce, and illness. Whatever the cause, if these feelings are not dealt with in a positive way, a child will begin to develop behavior problems and low self-esteem.

> Highlights some of the key milestones the company has accomplished. Communicates an action orientation and suggests that the business model can work.

Since its founding, FireFly has raised $110,000 in start-up capital, developed its first product line consisting of two inaugural toys (Jordo and the Comfort Kit), produced 500 product, and sold 126 Jordos and 75 Comfort Kits. Based on these results, FireFly is confident of its future growth potential.

4.1 The Products

> Testimonials or quotes add an emotional validation that FireFly has developed a product the customer will buy and use.

"My child wasn't willing to consider sleeping alone since her father died, but since we introduced Jordo, she has slept by herself for a whole two weeks."

"Jordo sleeps at the end of my bed at night and protects me."

Child, age 5

These testimonials speak to the power of toys to help children heal and communicate with their parents. FireFly has developed a bundled product line that can be sold together or independently. The Comfort Creature is a tactile plush fleece doll designed with special features that help children communicate their feelings. The Comfort Creature comes with a story book showing the Comfort Creature managing a life crisis (e.g., a death in the family). The Comfort Kit, intended to be sold separately, is a specially designed backpack filled with toys, crafts, games, and additional story books featuring the Comfort Creature. The activities in the Comfort Kits are designed to help the child and caregiver connect and deal with a life crisis. To that end, a caregiver's guide

> Product overview giving a sense of the FireFly's competitive advantage. It isn't just a plush toy; it is a bundled product (toy, book, caregiver's guide) that helps children in distress.

teaches parents/caregivers how to use the Comfort Creature, Comfort Kits and the story books to help the child deal with the situation. In addition, the company is upgrading its website to provide more resources for caregivers.

> The next section adds more detail about the product.

The Comfort Creatures

Comfort Creatures provide children with a plush animal with special features that help children express their feelings. Comfort Creatures, each paired with a story book, are plush animals with a special pocket in the belly called a "feelings pouch" and a secret compartment that opens in the back. The feelings pouch houses different pieces of fabric, such as soft fleece and scratchy sponge. Children use tactile objects to communicate their moods. Thus, a child

might touch the soft fleece to communicate the need for some warmth and security. In addition, the Creature's 24-inch tail wraps around the child as a portable hug. The first Comfort Creature is "Jordo."

> Pictures of the product powerfully communicate your concept.

> Description of product features drives home the customer value proposition: helping kids deal with trauma.

The Comfort Kits

Comfort Kits provide caregivers with toys, crafts, games, and books that help them help children through a difficult time. Each kit is accompanied by a guidebook for caregivers and specializes in different life challenges, such as divorce, death in the family, and nightmares. The guidebook provides caregivers with the tools to use the toys to help children work through these life situations. The first Comfort Kit is designed for children facing serious illness or death.

> The guidebook is the key component of FireFly's competitive advantage. The plan might go into more depth on how the guidebook adds value to caregivers.

FireFly has established relationships with toy companies that produce the products included in the Kits. We currently include Sculpey®, a polymer clay made by Polyform, a tone block provided by LP Rhythmics, chenille stems provided by Fibre Craft, and corn starch-based

> Outside relationships indicate the action orientation of FireFly. This shows the company is taking steps to execute its strategy.

noodles provided by Magic Nuudles™. FireFly worked in collaboration with FRIENDSWAY, a family grief center, to write "The Way of Play," the caregiver guide that provides activities, using the above products, to help caregivers connect to children, understand what the children feel, and nurture them through a difficult time. FireFly thus provides the expertise needed to use the products to help a child during a difficult time. At the same time, small toy manufacturers have a new distribution channel and application for their products.

FireFly's website (www.fireflytoys.com) is intended as a companion to the Kits. Soon the website will include resources for caregivers relating to our first issue, serious illness and death, and will provide chats online with a child psychologist to answer questions that caregivers may have about how to help their child/children.

> The website is intended to add further value to the customer, increasing the bundled nature of the product. Although the website adds to FireFly's competitive advantage, there are cost implications to building and maintaining the site. FireFly's pricing will have to take that into account.

4.2 Product Benefits

Comfort Creatures and Comfort Kits are:

> Bullets of product value proposition communicate why people will buy the product.

1. A product that helps children **gain relief** from the crisis they are facing.

2. An **affordable, straightforward solution** even an inexperienced caregiver can use to communicate effectively with a child going through a difficult life challenge.

3. **A creative way to communicate** with children at their own level and in their own time.

4. **An integrated system** of products that includes both the comforting toys for the child and the important advice for the caregiver. The products and advice specifically address the different educational and therapeutic challenges that both the caregiver and the children are facing.

FireFly Toys does more than provide comfort to the child. The Company also provides the comfort and the peace of mind to the caregivers that they are doing everything they can to support a child through a challenge or crisis.

Figure I *Competitive Map*

> Market research should support the dimensions shown on the axis as the key drivers of the purchase decision. In FireFly's case, the company has conducted focus groups with children and caregivers on what attributes they seek.

> The competitive map visually positions FireFly in the segment and highlights its competitive advantage.

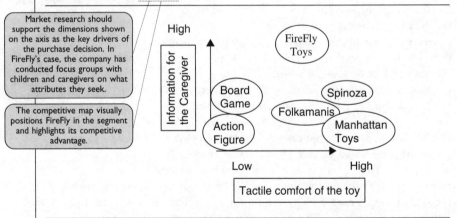

The competitive map (see Figure I) illustrates how the Comfort Creatures and Comfort Kits integrate the comfort of a plush toy with the information needed to connect to a child. Many products offer tactile comfort but lack directions on how to harness comfort and foster communication. As Figure I indicates, FireFly will be positioned to provide comfort to the child and expert information to caregivers.

4.3 Entry and Growth Strategy

FireFly will initially enter the market through hospitals, philanthropic organizations, and schools (institutions). After we have established these channels, we will expand to specialty retailers, e-commerce, and catalogues. The company will focus initial marketing efforts in Boston and New York. These cities have cohesive networks of child psychologists and caregivers in which the company has preestablished contacts.

> FireFly's entry strategy focuses on a few channels. It can test the product and learn from these channels before spending the money necessary to go after more channels.

> These channels help broaden its reach to the PTA.

The Company will target child life centers in New York– and Boston-area hospitals. These centers help ease children and families through the difficulties of hospital procedures. Initial partnerships are being developed with the child life centers at Dana Farber Cancer Institute and Tufts Medical Center.

> Geographic entry strategy. This will help the company and the reader understand the initial milestone the company plans to achieve. Limited entry also reduces the needed capital and expense associated with broader entry. It basically reduces the risk because if FireFly fails in its limited entry, the company will refine its strategy before burning additional capital.

Additionally, FireFly is testing the specialty retail channel. The Company has established sales relationships with two retailers: Edu-mart in Natick, MA, and Liberty House in New York, NY. The Company will work with specialty retailers that are more community-oriented and are seen as resources by caregivers. FireFly plans to host special events at the stores as a way to build relationships with the clients those stores serve.

> Although FireFly is focusing on the entry distribution channels at first, it is a good idea to test the growth strategy on a limited basis.

Once the Company is firmly established in New York and Boston, FireFly will use a controlled growth strategy to roll out to other geographic areas. Phase 2 will include Chicago and San Francisco, because the founder has lived and worked in these cities and can tap her network to facilitate entry into hospitals, philanthropic organizations, and schools in these cities.

> Geographic growth strategy.

> Although building on the founder's network increases validity in the idea, an investor might ask who these contacts are. To add credibility, FireFly should list names and organizational affiliations of these individuals.

Chapter Summary

The industry, customer, competition section sets the platform. The company and product section is the place to sell your story passionately. Communicate why you believe you have a compelling product. Tell us about its competitive advantage. Present a persuasive entry strategy followed by an exciting growth strategy. Whereas the foundation of most houses is cement and is buried underground, the house should show your style. Let your passion for the vision come through.

6 MARKETING PLAN: REACHING THE CUSTOMER

We have set the stage for your company to enter and grow in a marketplace successfully. Now we need to devise a strategy that will allow the company to reach its potential. Exhibit 6.1 highlights the major sections of the marketing plan. Let's look at each subsection in turn.

Target Market

Every marketing plan needs guiding principals. Based on the knowledge gleaned from the target market analysis, entrepreneurs need to position the product accordingly. All product strategies fall somewhere on a continuum stretching from rational purchases to emotional purchases. When one buys a new car, the rational purchase might be a low-cost reliable car such as the Ford Aspire. However, there is an emotional element as well: You want the car to be an extension of your personality. Thus, based on your economic means and self-perception, you buy a 1965 Ford Mustang convertible because of the emotional benefits it confers. Within every product space there is room for products at different points along the continuum. An entrepreneur needs to decide where his product fits (or where he would like to position it) as this influences the other aspects of the marketing plan.

Exhibit 6.1 *Marketing Plan*

- The target market strategy
- The product/service strategy
- Pricing strategy
- Distribution strategy
- Advertising and promotion
- Sales strategy
- Sales and marketing forecasts.

FireFly, for instance, tends toward the emotional side of the continuum. Parents and caregivers do not really need to purchase the toy but believe that by doing so they will improve a child's well-being.

Rational ← X FireFly Emotional →

Product/Service Strategy

Building from the target market strategy, this section of the plan describes how your product is differentiated from the competition. It's informative to look back on the competitive dimensions you described in the competitive profile matrix. What attributes are important to the customers? Are they willing to pay a premium for those features? Will they continue to pay that premium? One of the biggest mistakes entrepreneurs make is evaluating an opportunity as if it were static. But marketplaces change; customer values change. With cell phones, in the early years people paid huge premiums for the hardware and the minutes. As the product became more widely dispersed, price became an increasingly important attribute. Today wireless companies give away the hardware and entice customers with great calling plans. The point is that if you had entered the market early and viewed it in a static fashion, falling prices would have caught you by surprise and potentially led to your firm's demise. As you think about your product/service strategy, try to identify the attributes that have the potential to be sustainable. What will the customer value over the long run?

You will have to consider other issues as well. Discuss why the customer will switch to your product and how you will retain customers so that they don't switch to your competition in the future. This section also should address how you will provide service to the customer. What type of technical support will you provide? Will you offer warrantees? What kinds of product upgrades will be available and when? It is important to detail all these efforts, as they must all be accounted for in the pricing of the product. Many times entrepreneurs underestimate the costs of these services, and this can lead to a drain on cash flow and can ultimately lead to bankruptcy.

Pricing Strategy

Determining how to price your product is always difficult. The two primary approaches are the cost-plus approach and the market-demand approach. We advise entrepreneurs to avoid cost-plus pricing. It is difficult to determine your actual cost accurately, especially if this is a new venture with a limited history. New ventures consistently underestimate the true cost of developing their products. For example, how much did it really cost to write that software? The cost would include salaries and the payroll tax burden, computers and other assets, the overhead contribution, and so on. Since most entrepreneurs underestimate these costs,[1] there is a tendency to underprice the product. Another pricing strategy that gets entrepreneurs in trouble is to offer a low price so that they can penetrate the market and gain market share rapidly. The problems with a low price are that it may be difficult to raise the price later, demand at that price may overwhelm your ability to produce the product in sufficient volume, and it may strain cash flow. Also, a low price may connote lower value versus the competition. Therefore, the better method is to canvass the market and determine an appropriate price based on what the competition is offering and how your product is positioned. If you are offering a low-cost product, price below market rates. If your product is of better quality or has features superior to those of the competition (the more common case), it should be priced above market rates.

---

[1]The fluid nature of a start-up firm means that purchasing power, changing product or service components, and even the offering make the real and total cost of a product very difficult to pin down.

Distribution Strategy

This section identifies how you will reach the customer. Many new ventures assume the availability and capacity of channels of distribution for a new "improved" product. That's almost always a mistake. One of the authors had a friend who developed chili in a jar. That entrepreneur had extensive experience in packaged foods, previously having worked for a large national food conglomerate and then with a successful beverage start-up. Although the product was of high quality (as good as making it from scratch and much better than chili in a can), the entrepreneur found it impossible to break into the grocery store distribution channel in a significant way. The large food processors controlled all the shelf space. Even though the product was new and improved, it did not survive.

It is also important to understand the cost of reaching the customer even if you can access the distribution channels. The e-commerce boom of the late 1990s assumed that the growth in Internet usage and purchases would create new demand for pure Internet companies, yet the distribution strategy for many of those firms did not make sense. Pets.com and other online pet supply firms had a strategy where the pet owner would log on, order the product from the site, and then receive delivery via UPS or the U.S. Postal Service. In theory this works, except that the price the market would bear for this product didn't cover the exorbitant shipping costs for a 40-pound bag of dog food.

It is wise to examine how the customer currently acquires the product. If your customer buys dog food at Wal-Mart, you probably should use primarily traditional retail outlets to sell a new brand of dog food. This is not to say that entrepreneurs may not develop a multichannel distribution strategy, but if they want to achieve maximum growth, at some point they will have to use common distribution techniques or reeducate the customer about the buying process (which can be very expensive). If you determine that Wal-Mart is the best distribution channel, the next question is, Can you access it? For a new start-up in dog food it may be difficult to get shelf space at Wal-Mart. That may suggest an entry strategy of boutique pet stores to build brand recognition. The key here is to identify appropriate channels and then assess how costly it is to access them.

FireFly is using a distribution strategy similar to that of Spinoza Bears to enter the market. Toys are a very competitive industry, and access to large distribution channels such as Wal-Mart and Toys R Us is virtually impossible for a new small company. These large distribution channels demand steep discounts, guaranteed sales, and large volumes. Thus, Fire-Fly is trying to build relationships with hospitals, philanthropic organizations, and schools because those channels enable it to command a higher price. The clients of these outlets are also FireFly's likely customers. It remains to be seen whether FireFly's strategy will prove successful, but recognizing how difficult it is to tap existing channels has the company going in the right direction.

Advertising and Promotion

Communicating effectively with your customer requires advertising and promotion. Referring again to the dot-com boom of the late 1990s, the defunct Computer.com made a classic mistake in its attempt to build brand recognition. It blew over half the venture capital it raised on a series of expensive Super Bowl ads for the January 2000 event ($3 million of $5.8 million raised on three Super Bowl ads).[2] Resource-constrained entrepreneurs need to select the appropriate strategies carefully. What avenues most effectively reach your primary target audience (PTA)? If you can identify your PTA by name, direct mail may be more effective. Try to utilize grassroots techniques such as public relations efforts geared toward mainstream media. Sheri Poe, the founder of Ryka shoes, a company geared toward women, appeared on the *Oprah Winfrey* show, touting shoes for women designed by women. The response was overwhelming. In fact, she was so besieged by demand, she couldn't supply enough shoes.

It is important to distinguish between early-stage advertising strategies and those which will emerge as the company grows. For example, one of the authors was on the founding team for Jiffy Lube. In the early days the company used direct mail (coupons) to all registered vehicle owners. As the company grew nationally, it switched to radio advertisements because people listened to the radio when they were driving and were more likely to think about the need for an oil change. The key is to develop an appropriate strategy based on your PTA and the stage of the company's development.

---

[2]O. Sacribey, "Private Companies Temper IPO Talk," *IPO Reporter*, Dec. 18, 2000.

As you develop a multipronged advertising and promotion strategy, create detailed schedules that show which avenues you will pursue and the associated costs. These types of schedules serve many purposes, including providing accurate cost estimates, which will help in assessing how much capital you need to raise. These schedules also build credibility in the eyes of potential investors as they show that you understand the nuances of your industry.

Sales Strategy

This section provides the backbone that supports all of the parts described above. Specifically, it illustrates what kind and level of human capital you will devote to the effort. How many salespeople and how much customer support do you need? Will these people be internal to the organization or outsourced? If they are internal, will there be a designated sales force or will different members of the company serve in a sales capacity at different times? This section builds credibility if the entrepreneur demonstrates an understanding of how the business should operate.

Sales and Marketing Forecasts

Gauging the impact of these efforts is difficult. Nonetheless, to build a compelling story, entrepreneurs need to show projections of revenues well into the future. How do you derive these numbers? There are two methods: the comparable method and the build-up method. The comparable method models sales forecasts after what other companies have achieved, adjusting for the age of the company, variances in product attributes, support services such as advertising and promotion, and so on. After detailed investigation of the industry and market, entrepreneurs know the competitive players and have a good understanding of their history. In essence, the entrepreneur monitors a number of comparable competitors and then explains why her business varies from those models.

Based on the comparable method, FireFly's projected sales (see section 5.7 of the plan, below) of 23,000 units (both Creatures and Kits) in year 1 seems aggressive. Referring back to the competitive matrix table in Chapter 3, we see that Folkmanis has sales of $2.2 million and Spinoza has sales of $1 million (we left out Manhattan Toys because it is much larger and carries multiple lines). That would mean that Folkmanis has a volume of at least 22,000 units per year (assuming all units are sold at the highest price) and that Spinoza has sales of at least 5,000 units per year. FireFly is expecting to match that level almost immediately. Considering that FireFly is planning to use the same distribution strategy as Spinoza, investors should be highly skeptical of FireFly's predictions.

In the build-up method, the entrepreneur identifies all the revenue sources and then estimates how much of that revenue type it can generate per day or some other small period. The build-up technique is an imprecise method for a new start-up with a limited operating history, but it is critically important to assess the viability of the opportunity, so important, in fact, that we advise entrepreneurs to use both the comparable and the build-up techniques to assess how well they converge. If the two methods are widely divergent, go back through and try to determine why. The deep knowledge you gain of your business model will help you articulate the opportunity to stakeholders as well as manage the business when it is launched.

We can use the build-up method to validate FireFly's projections. The company is estimating sales of approximately $700,000 in year 1 and $4.3 million in year 2 (see Tables 5.3 and 5.4 in the business plan). FireFly is using a direct sale force consisting of one person in year 1 and three in year 2. That equates to $700,000 per salesperson in year 1 and $1.4 million per salesperson in year 2. That seems high. To compare, we looked at the *Business Week* small business website that provides benchmark comparisons.[3] Small businesses in the durable wholesale sector average approximately $200,000 per employee. It appears that FireFly is underestimating its headcount in both years. Although the year 1 figures are close to the benchmark, it is likely that FireFly will be less efficient in the first year. Thus, you might expect FireFly to perform worse than the benchmark number. Year 2 sales per employee is 250 percent higher than the industry benchmark.

We also can look at a benchmark company, the Vermont Teddy Bear Company (VTBC). In 2001 VTBC had sales of $37 million and employed

---

[3]http://www.businessweek.com/smallbiz/bizminer/bizminer.htm.

338 people. Many of the employees (167 people) were in production. Considering that FireFly is outsourcing production, we reduce VTBC's headcount by its production employees and are left with 171 people. VTBC reports that 142 of those employees are in marketing. Once again, FireFly's projections seem overly optimistic. Even if we look at year 5, when FireFly might achieve economies of scale, its projected sales per employee are over three times those of VTBC. Something has to give. Either FireFly needs to hire more people over time or it has to revise its sales downward.

	Sales	Sales-people	Sales/Sales-person	Employees	Sales/Employee
FireFly Yr 1	$700	1	$700,000	3	$250,000
FireFly Yr 2	$4.3M	3	$1.4M	6	$716,000
FireFly Yr 5	$24M	32	$750,000	38	$632,000
Business Week					$200,000
Vermont Teddy Bears	$37M	142	$260,500	171	$216,000

The one thing we know for certain is that these forecasts will never be 100 percent accurate, and so the question is the degree of error. Detailed investigation of comparable companies reduces that error. Triangulating the comparable results with the build-up results reduces that error further. The smaller the error is, the less likely it is that the company will run out of cash. Also, rigorous estimates build an intimate understanding of the forces that will affect revenue and credibility with the investors. Although FireFly's projections seem optimistic, this is pretty common. Entrepreneurs always believe things will happen more quickly and with less cost than is typically the case. We expect that in future iterations of the plan FireFly will develop stronger projections based on investor and distribution channel feedback. Nonetheless, going through these exercises gives you the ammunition to convince investors and others that your projections are reasonable.

FireFly Marketing Plan

5.0 THE MARKETING PLAN

5.1 Target Market Strategy

"Parents feel tremendous guilt because they feel they're spreading themselves too thin," says Dr. Joshua Sparrow of Children's Hospital in Boston.[1] Thus, they want to optimize the time they have with their children, especially during tough times. Caregivers are always looking for new products that will make it easier to communicate with a child. Comfort Creatures and Comfort Kits fulfill this need. They help caregivers connect with children in distress.

> Positions FireFly toward the emotional purchase end of the continuum. Emotional purchasers tend to be less price-sensitive, justifying premium pricing.

> This kind of suggestive comment carries far more credibility if it is supported with evidence such as an industry trade article.

5.2 Product Strategy

The Comfort Creatures and Comfort Kits integrate the comfort of a plush toy with the information needed to connect to a child. Many competing products offer tactile comfort but lack directions on how to harness comfort and foster communication. FireFly will be positioned to provide comfort to the child and expertise and information to caregivers.

> The nature of the FireFly business model, selling a low-tech product, doesn't require much after-sale service or support. Thus, this section doesn't need to address those issues.

> States FireFly's competitive advantage.

5.3 Pricing Strategy

The retail pricing for the Comfort Creature is $40 per unit. Most other plush toys and dolls of the same size retail for $20 per unit, while plush toys with therapeutic features fetch $100 or more (Spinoza Bear). Comfort creatures come in at a much more competitive price while still at a premium over basic dolls. The pricing was validated by focus groups and child-care professionals.

> Price is based on competition and focus group feedback. Once FireFly enters more distribution channels, it will have a better gauge on what price its products can demand.

> An addendum summarizing focus group data and referenced comments from child-care professionals would add credibility here.

The Comfort Kits will retail for $65 per unit. This price was chosen by comparing the features and contents of other all-inclusive kits to those of the Comfort Kit. Comfort Kits' superior features warrant a premium over the $35 to $40 price of other kits.

5.4 Distribution Strategy

FireFly will enter the market through hospitals, philanthropic organizations, schools, and direct sales to caregivers. As the company grows, it will expand to

---

[1]Jeffrey Kluger and Alice Park, "The Quest for a Super Kid," *Time South Pacific*, April 30, 2001, Issue 17, p. 48.

an e-commerce website, specialty toy stores, catalogues, and direct sales via trade shows, conferences, and special events.

The Company has established relationships with Dana Farber Cancer Institute and Tufts Medical Center. Both organizations have tentatively agreed to provide Comfort Creatures and Comfort Kits to their patients. FireFly is working on a training seminar to be delivered to caregivers in these organizations.

Partnerships with philanthropists are being developed to deliver the Comfort Creatures and Kits to children or programs in need. Philanthropists will purchase the products for children in programs they want to support. These partnerships not only will provide the children and caregivers with valuable tools for communication but also will build the awareness of the FireFly brand among the people who volunteer and run these organizations and philanthropic events. Initial relationships have been established with the Pan Massachusetts Challenge, a 3-day bike ride to raise money for the Dana Farber Institute in Boston, and FRIENDS WAY, a family grief center in Providence, Rhode Island. At the August 2002 event, FireFly donated a number of Comfort Creatures and Comfort Kits to the Pan Massachusetts Challenge and also had a booth at the finish line where the product was sold to interested participants. We will continue to develop these channels in both Boston and New York.

FireFly has conducted focus groups at several schools to test how children interact with the products. The positive results suggest that schools will be a viable distribution channel. The Lemberg Preschool at Brandeis University, the Wimphfeimer Nursery School at Vassar College, and the Lab School at the University of Chicago have expressed interest in using Comfort Creatures and Comfort Kits.

After the Company grows, it will expand to specialty retailers that sell educational or therapeutic toys. To learn more about these distribution channels, the Company will attend conferences such as the Association for Play Therapy Conference as well as trade shows such as Toy Fair.

5.5 Advertising and Promotion

In the first year, the focus of the advertising campaign will target professional caregivers in the following five areas:

1. Special events
2. Specialty store workshops
3. Public relations efforts

4. Newsletter, e-letter, magazine advertising
5. Website

> Nice visual that summarizes advertising activity. It also helps build the financial projections. These figures appear in the income statement.

Table 5.1 *Advertising Budget and Timeline Over Year 1*

Promotional Tools	Timetable	Budget Over 1 Year
Special Events	One a month	$24,000
Specialty toy store workshops	One a month	$6,000
PR	Ongoing	$12,000

> The plan should list the exact magazines it plans on using. That can be accomplished in a footnote or directly in the chart.

Promotional Tools	Timetable	Budget Over 1 Year
Newsletter, e-letter, and magazine advertising	10 ads in regional mags, November, December, February, April, June, August	**Mags:** $7,000/each = $70,000
	12 ads in early childhood newsletters, November, December, January, April, May	**Newsletters:** $300/each = $3,600
Website	Ongoing	$20,000
Total costs		**$135,600**

> Note that this ties to the income statement: $115,600 for advertising plus $20,000 for the website.

1. Special Events

Conferences and trade shows will serve as key launch pads for new products and will build awareness of the FireFly brand. The company will attend both industry shows, such as the Toy Fair, and topic-specific conferences, such as the National Grief and Families conference. At the topic-specific shows FireFly will be a vendor but also will work to partner with presenters who are focusing on loss, divorce, or other life difficulties. The Company's management team will attend training conferences of child therapists and child life service providers. These conferences, many required by state education boards, will allow the company to connect to caregivers and better understand their needs.

> Notice how FireFly has identified venues that reach its core customer: caregivers of children in distress.

2. Specialty Store Workshops

FireFly plans on testing specialty store workshops at their locations in regard to difficult parenting issues, alerting

> $6000 is a low-cost test to investigate how to enter the specialty store channel most effectively. Money well spent.

parents to the benefits of FireFly's products. At these events FireFly will share information about best practices and demonstrate how to use the Company's products. FireFly products will be sold at these events.

3. PR with National Opinion Leaders

> Showing achievements adds credibility and shows that FireFly knows how to get free PR.

> Showing the actual articles in the appendix supports the credibility of the plan.

FireFly has already received significant public relations coverage, including articles in *Time* magazine, the *Boston Business Journal*, the *Boston Metro*, *Metro West Daily News*, *Where* magazine, and *CareerJournal* from the *Wall Street Journal*. FireFly is continuing its PR effort by identifying opinion leaders that will lend credibility and provide marketing support for the Company's products and brand. To do this the Company is targeting specific individuals whom parents, caregivers, and philanthropic organizations trust. For example, we will approach *Oprah Winfrey*, *Good Morning America*, the *Wall Street Journal*, Nickelodeon, and leading child psychologists.

4. Newsletter, E-letter, and Magazine Advertising

> Demonstrates that FireFly has done its homework. It knows which outlets reach its core customer.

Caregivers rely on newsletters and magazines as sources of information about what to buy children during a difficult time. Publications that reach the target customer include:

- The distribution lists at child-care programs and institutions
- *Parenting* magazine
- Parents' newsletters
- The Association of the Education of Young Children newsletter

Caregivers will be able to sign up for FireFly's quarterly e-newsletter that highlights new product offerings and tips about particular topics. Staff at these sources would be given product for evaluation purposes. The company also will work to get the products evaluated by trusted journals such as *Parents Choice*.

5. The Website:

> Every new company needs a website and Web strategy today. These are low-cost venues to supplement the overall advertising and promotion strategy.

The website will provide access to information, expertise, and product. Caregivers will be able to order product as well as find links to other important sites that will help their children through their difficult situations. The Company will work with nationally recognized organizations to link the website to their sites and vice versa. The website will offer stories of caregivers and children, product descriptions, and connections to therapy resources. FireFly is in talks with the Dougy Center, an

> Strategic relationships can multiply the numbers of people you come into contact with.

organization that provides support to grieving children and families, about linking its website to FireFly's website. This partnership would provide links to grief centers across the United States. The company also is designing a recognizable image to put on other websites to allow other sites to link to ours easily.

5.6 Sales Strategy

In year 1 Megan MacDonald, Director of Marketing, along with the Sales Director (to be hired once the next round of financing is closed) and the founder, Lauren McLaughlin, will focus on establishing contacts with hospitals, philanthropic organizations, and schools. As FireFly grows, it will hire more sales personnel to manage the existing sales channels and grow distribution into the specialty store channel. Table 5.2 shows the headcount buildout.

> Table is useful in that it ties directly to financial projections and facilitates reality checks. As discussed above, it appears that FireFly is understaffing for the sales it is projecting.

Table 5.2 *Marketing/Sales Headcount*

	Year 1	Year 2	Year 3	Year 4	Year 5
Marketing director	1	1	1	1	1
	($45,000)	($55,000)	($65,000)	($75,000)	($90,000)
Sales director	1	1	1	1	1
	($50,000)	($60,000)	($65,000)	($75,000)	($90,000)
Sales staff		2	15	25	40
		($126,000)	($1.1M)	($2M)	($3.5M)
Total headcount	2	4	17	27	42
	($95,000)	($241,000)	($1.23M)	($2.15M)	($3.68M)

5.7 Sales Forecast

FireFly Toys will experience rapid growth in its first 5 years. To facilitate this growth, the Company will be entering new distribution channels each year with new product introductions.

In the first year the Company projects sales of almost 17,000 units of Comfort Creatures and 5,000 units of Comfort Kits. The monthly projected sales for years 1 and 2 are shown in Tables 5.3 and 5.4. Note that the price is the average weighted price based on sales to the three different channels.

> Projections seem too aggressive, much higher than industry benchmark, as discussed above.

Table 5.3 Comfort Creature Unit Sales and Revenue		
	Year 1	Year 2
Sept	100	4,000
Oct	200	6,000
Nov	600	7,500
Dec	900	9,000
Jan	1,300	5,500
Feb	1,400	5,500
Mar	1,700	5,500
Apr	1,700	7,000
May	1,750	9,000
Jun	2,250	6,000
Jul	2,300	7,000
Aug	2,700	9,000
Total units	16,900	81,000
Price	$31	$29
Total revenue	$527,280	$2,342,520

Table 5.4 Comfort Kits Unit Sales and Revenue		
	Year 1	Year 2
Sept	50	2,000
Oct	75	2,500
Nov	150	3,000
Dec	300	3,500
Jan	400	2,500
Feb	500	2,500
Mar	500	3,000
Apr	500	3,000
May	500	4,500
Jun	700	3,000
Jul	725	4,500
Aug	600	6,000
Total units	5,000	40,000
Price	$52	$51
Total revenue	$259,750	$2,024,800

Chapter Summary

Many people consider the marketing plan the most important part of the planning process because it communicates how you will reach the customer. As we discuss later in the book, reaching the customer is often the most critical risk a new venture faces. Investors will look at this part of the plan to see if you have a credible strategy. That means looking at the distribution channels, pricing, and advertising plans. The more detail you provide, the more credibility you build. Liberally use tables to highlight advertising outlets and costs, sales and marketing headcounts, and salaries. Spend the time to get these details right because it means that you will have a stronger grasp on your major operating expenses and your road to profitability.

7 OPERATIONS AND DEVELOPMENT: EXECUTION

Operations Plan

The operations section of the plan has been shortened as more companies have outsourced nonvital aspects of production. Exhibit 7.1 illustrates the main sections of the operations plan. The key is to articulate operational competitive advantages and address how operations will provide value to your customers. This section also details the production cycle, allowing the entrepreneur to gauge the impact on working capital. When does the company pay for inputs? How long does it take to produce the product? When does the customer buy the product, and, more important, when does the customer pay for the product? The time from the beginning of this process until the product is paid for will drain cash flow and has implications for financing. From the FireFly business plan we see that it needs to make a 50 percent down payment five months before it receives the product. Add to that the time before it may receive payment from its distribution channels and you can see how many rapidly growing new companies run out of cash even though they have increasing sales. Therefore, it is crucial to finance properly the time cash is tied up in the procurement, production, sales, and receivables cycle.

Exhibit 7.1 *Operations Plan*

- Operations strategy
- Scope of operations
- Ongoing operations

Another factor that has cash implications is whether the operations strategy is to "buy" or "build" the production process. For instance, if FireFly built a manufacturing facility, it would cost a lot of money. Instead, FireFly buys production, moving those expenses to variable costs as opposed to fixed costs. How do you make the decision whether to buy or build? First, what is your competitive advantage? If it lies in how you put the product together, it probably makes sense to build. For instance, Dell derives its advantage by customizing its personal computers (PCs). Thus, it needs a facility to assemble its product. You also may build if your advantage lies in some proprietary technology that you need to keep close control of (although you may only need to make the component where your technology is embedded). Otherwise, consider buying, which means outsourcing the operations, because the second key factor here is the cost. Building often means huge fixed expenditures up front; this means raising more capital, diluting your equity, and lengthening the time to break even. Basically it means increased risk.

Operations Strategy

The first subsection provides a strategy overview. How does your business win/compare on the dimensions of cost, quality, timeliness, and flexibility? The emphasis should be on the aspects that provide your venture with a comparative advantage. FireFly is producing its products in China, which equates to lower costs of production. That is a comparative advantage vis-à-vis a few of its competitors, but it is likely that many competitors also outsource to lower-cost locations. Thus, this section can be short and concise because operations is not contributing to the company's competitive advantage.

It is also appropriate to discuss the geographic location of production facilities and how this enhances the firm's competitive advantage. Discuss available labor, local regulations, transportation, infrastructure, proximity to suppliers, and so forth. The section also should provide a description of the facilities, how the facilities will be acquired (bought or leased), and how future growth will be handled (e.g., renting adjoining buildings).

Scope of Operations

What is the production process for your product or service? A diagram powerfully illustrates how your company adds value to the various inputs. Constructing the diagram also facilitates making the decision which production aspects to keep in-house (build) and which to outsource (buy). Because cash flow is king and resource-constrained new ventures typically should minimize fixed expenses on production facilities, the general rule is to outsource as much production as possible. However, as was discussed above, there is a major caveat to that rule. Your venture should control aspects of production that are central to your competitive advantage. FireFly's competitive advantage lies in design and marketing. The actual production of the plush animals and kits can be outsourced easily. Outsourcing the aspects that aren't proprietary reduces fixed costs for production equipment and facility expenditures, and that means that you have to raise less money and give up less equity. Since most of the operations for FireFly are outsourced, there isn't a need to discuss this in the subsection on scope of operations.

The scope of operations also should discuss partnerships with vendors, suppliers, partners, and so on. Again, the diagram should illustrate the supplier and vendor relationships by category (or by name if the list isn't too long and you already have identified your suppliers). The diagram helps you visualize the various relationships and ways to manage them better or eliminate them. The operations diagram also helps entrepreneurs identify personnel needs. For example, the diagram provides an indication of how many production workers might be needed depending on the hours of operations, number of shifts, and so forth.

Ongoing Operations

This section builds on the scope of operations by providing details on day-to-day activities. How many units will be produced in a day, and what kinds of inputs are necessary? An operating cycle overview diagram graphically illustrates the impact of production on cash flow. As entrepreneurs complete this detail, they can start to establish performance parameters, which will help monitor and modify the production process into the future and test assumptions regarding competitive advantages. If this is an operational business plan, the level of detail may include specific job descriptions, but in the typical business plan this level of detail would be much more than an investor would need or want to see in the initial evaluation phase. Since FireFly is still early in its development, it doesn't include a fully detailed operations plan.

FireFly Operations Plan

6.0 OPERATIONS PLAN

> FireFly outsources production because its competitive advantage comes from product design and marketing. The key is to produce a high-quality product at a low cost. Hence, they partner with a reputable manufacturer's rep who handles the low-cost production in Asia.

> This is the first mention of being socially conscious. If it's worth saying in the operations plan, it's worth discussing in the mission or marketing plan.

> Notice how Exhibit 6.1 identifies the timing of activity, including when payments will be made. It also shows which functions are FireFly's primary responsibilities and which are The Five of Us's responsibilities.

> This diagram also helps you evaluate the operations process. For example, why does it take so long to get a prototype built? Is there some way to speed that cycle? It takes 7 weeks to receive, review, and redo the prototype. That seems to lack a sense of urgency. This cycle is probably based on FireFly's first run of Jordos. The question Lauren should be asking is, can we shorten this for future runs? The old adage holds that time is money.

6.1 Operations Strategy

All manufacturing will be outsourced. The company works with The Five of Us, a toy company based in San Francisco with manufacturing operations in China. They have facilitated our initial manufacturing of product. They work with factories that do not use slave or child labor and that pay and treat their workers well, adding to FireFly's image as a socially conscious company.

The product designs are based on ideas conceived in-house. The process from design to retail is 9 months for new Comfort Creatures. Exhibit 6.1 demonstrates the typical operations cycle.

Exhibit 6.1 The Operations Cycle

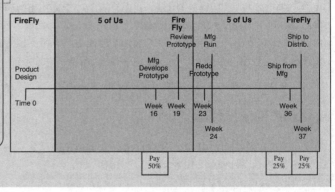

The Five of Us requires a minimum order of 500 units. The payment terms are 50% upfront, 25% on shipment, and 25% upon arrival. FireFly will work with other manufacturers as the manufacturing needs increase. The production cycle, typical for the toy industry, should not change when other manufacturers are used.

> We would like to see validation that this is typical for the toy industry. It seems that this may be a function of FireFly's small size and low negotiation power. As the company grows, we would expect that it will be able to improve terms.

Development Plan

The development plan highlights the process of preparing the company for generating sales and provides a detailed timeline. Exhibit 7.2 highlights the main sections of the development plan. Many new ventures will require a significant level of effort and time to launch the product or service. This section explains how the business will progress from its current position to becoming a going concern. For example, new software or hardware products often require months of development. The development plan should detail the steps taken to get to that developed software product.

Development Strategy

What work remains to be completed? What factors need to come together for development to be successful? What risks to development does the firm face? For example, software development is notorious for taking longer and costing more than most companies imagined. Detailing the necessary work and what is required for the work to be considered successful helps entrepreneurs understand and manage the risks involved. After you have laid out these details, a development timeline is assembled.

Exhibit 7.2 Development Plan

- Development strategy
- Development timeline

Development Timeline

A development timeline is a schedule that highlights major milestones and can be used to monitor progress and make changes. The timeline helps entrepreneurs track major events and schedule activities to execute those events. It also provides a guidepost of promised accomplishments for the investors. FireFly adds a headcount table in this section. Headcount tables in the appropriate section suggest that you understand your infrastructure needs. In this case the table is somewhat redundant with the one in the marketing plan as it includes marketing employees again. Nonetheless, we like to see this level of detail because it suggests a level of understanding and ties directly to the costs in the financial statements.

FireFly Development Plan

7.0 DEVELOPMENT PLAN

FireFly has developed its first product line. The "Jordo" Comfort Creature and associated books deal with death in the family and serious illness. The Comfort Kits provide activities that support the Jordo plush animal. FireFly's website is functioning but needs upgrading. In the coming year FireFly will create a solid sales force training program and launch its second product line. FireFly also will work to build strong relationships with philanthropic organizations and individuals who are influencers in those organizations.

> Section briefly lays out initiatives, which then are illustrated in timeline. Note how FireFly starts by pointing out the initial production run. This statement communicates that the company is active and meeting milestones (it has successfully designed and produced its initial products).

7.1 Development Strategy

FireFly has manufactured an initial product run of 500 Comfort Creatures (called "Jordo") and Comfort Kits. This limited run confirms that The 5 of Us is a reliable partner. Once the Company closes the next round of financing, a larger production run of 25,000 Jordos and 5,000 Comfort Kits will commence. The company is working to develop additional products within these lines. These include a new Comfort Creature named "Mooshi" and the next Comfort Kit for children coping with divorce.

The website for the company has been completed, and sales have begun. The next phase will be to upgrade the website and enable online transactions. The company's strategy is to focus on four primary initiatives:

> Having website sales is very significant, but including the volume would add further impact.

> The use of bullet points creates a visual that draws the reader's attention.

- Sales to large institutions such as hospitals and hospices
- Inventory management and fulfillment
- Building an internal management and sales infrastructure
- Increasing efforts to develop a specialty store distribution channel

The timeline and staffing schedule are shown in Exhibit 7.1.

> The timeline visually represents when major tasks will be initiated and completed.

Exhibit 7.1 Development Timeline

Activity	Aug-02	Sep-02	Oct-02	Nov-02	Dec-02	Jan-03	Feb-03	Mar-03	Apr-03	May-03	Jun-03	Jul-03	Aug-03	Sep-03
Received 1st 500 creatures	■													
Develop institutional sales channel			■	■	■	■	■	■	■					
Close Round B of financing for $320K					■									
Develop 2nd Comfort Creature (Mooshi)						■	■	■	■	■				
25,000 production run Jordo Creature							■							
5,000 production run Kits							■							
Increase website functionality														
Hire sales director								■	■					
Develop specialty store channel								■	■	■	■	■	■	■
Hire operations director									■					
15,000 production run of Jordo Creature										■	■	■	■	
30,000 production run of Comfort Kits										■	■	■	■	
15,000 production run of Mooshi Creature												■	■	■

Headcount table illustrates how the company will build out its infrastructure. Many new companies underestimate personnel costs. A headcount table helps improve accuracy.

However, one of the inevitable questions raised in a start-up firm is the pay for the founding management team. Will you pay market salaries, or will the founding management team be given equity incentives? In Exhibit 7.2 it appears the CEO (Lauren McLaughlin) will be working for below-market wages for the first few years with a pretty dramatic ramp-up by year 5. This seems logical and is obviously doable because Lauren is the CEO and won't take money that isn't there. The product design executive salary doesn't seem realistic. He or she enters the firm in year 3 at what appears to be below-market wages (why else would you increase pay 40 percent the next year and 20 percent in the following year?). Same with the marketing director.

Exhibit 7.2 *Staffing Plan*

	Year 1	Year 2	Year 3	Year 4	Year 5
CEO	1	1	1	1	1
	($45,000)	($80,000)	($100,000)	($120,000)	($250,000)
COO					1
					($250,000)
Accounting		1	1	1	1
		($40,000)	($45,000)	($45,000)	($65,000)
Office admin					1
					($65,000)
Product design			1	1	1
			($70,000)	($100,000)	($120,000)
Operations director	1	1	1	1	1
	($45,000)	($55,000)	($65,000)	($75,000)	($90,000)
Marketing director			1	1	1
			($95,000)	($150,000)	($200,000)
Sales director	1	1	1	1	1
	($30,000)	($75,000)	($95,000)	($150,000)	($200,000)
Sales staff		2	8	16	30
		($130,000)	($600,000)	($1.36M)	($2.85M)
Consultants	($60,000)	(100,000)	($175,000)	($240,000)	($340,000)
Total headcount	3	6	14	22	38
	($180,000)	($480,000)	($1.245M)	($2.24M)	($4.39M)

Chapter Summary

Although the operations and development plans tend to be shorter in the standard business plan format, these sections deserve attention and will be considerably longer if you are writing an operational business plan for internal use. The activities covered in these sections have direct cost implications. The more homework you do, the better you will be able to plan your cash flow. This has direct implications for the amount of capital you will need to raise and how you will make strategic decision once you launch. Even if you are outsourcing most of the production of your product, you need to spend time understanding the operational process so that you can evaluate and choose the most appropriate partner. Making a bad choice of a production partner will have potentially large cost and time implications; make sure you have the deep understanding needed.

The development plan is also an important exercise. Planning all the details needed to launch a business is imperative to success. In Chapter 2 we provided you with the Business Plan Guide, which is basically a template to lay out all the actions you need to take. As you go through the marketing plan and the operations plan, you should be able to fill in more details that need to happen during the launch phase. Tim DeMello, serial founder of Wall Street Games and Streamline, shared with students at Babson College an exercise he uses to identify all the necessary actions that need to be taken. Tim had every member of his founding team sit in a room with flip chart sheets taped to the walls. The team members then went around the room, writing down actions. A second cycle added detailed actions that supported the major actions identified in the first round. They continued in this manner until they exhausted new action items. Then the actions were organized along a timeline, and responsibilities were given to the appropriate team members. Although we don't recommend showing that level of detail in your development timeline, the deep learning you gain by going through the process will be invaluable and help you make sound decisions going forward.

8 TEAM: THE KEY TO SUCCESS

George Doriot, the father of venture capital and the founder of American Research and Development Corporation (the first modern-day venture capital firm), said that he would rather "back an 'A' entrepreneur with a 'B' idea than a 'B' entrepreneur with an 'A' idea." He reasoned that an A team can mold and reshape a B idea into a winning opportunity more easily than a B team can execute an A idea. Therefore, the team section of the business plan is often the section professional investors read after examining the executive summary. Thus, it is critical that the plan depict the members responsible for key activities and convey the idea that they are exceptional people with integrity, knowledge and skills.

In many cases the business planning process will help you identify the gaps that exist on your team. It is rare for a founding entrepreneur to have all the competencies needed to launch a successful business. In fact, research suggests that ventures launched by teams are more likely to become sustainable businesses than are those launched by individuals. One study found that over 83 percent of companies that achieved sales of $5 million or more were started by teams, whereas just over half the companies launched by teams failed.[1] As you complete different sections of the plan, especially the marketing, operations, and development plans, start thinking about what kind of skills you need to execute those activities successfully. For example, we work with many bright engineers who understand technology and know how to create sophisticated de-

---

[1]Arnold Cooper and Albert Bruno: "Success Among High Technology Firms." *Business Horizons,* April 8, 1977, p. 20.

vices or software but lack the business skills necessary to launch a viable business, such as business development, sales, and finance. We also work with lots of sharp businesspeople who have identified a customer need but don't have the technology background to build a prototype. In these situations it makes sense to recruit a cofounder, someone who complements your skill set so that together you can fill the gaps.

However, you can't fill out a team right from the beginning. That would drain too much cash (assuming you paid them) and dilute too much equity. You need to be strategic and think about the two to five key people you will need to succeed. You also have to anticipate when you will need them. At FireFly the core team is Lauren and Megan. They cover enough of the core skills to build the product, test the market, and establish the distribution channels. As the company starts to grow, a likely need is someone with strong operations and logistics skills. Even though the company intends to outsource, it needs somebody to manage the overseas producer and the distribution to its channels. Fossa Medical, the other company we highlight in this book, started with two core team members, Gloria Ro Kolb, who provides the business, product design, and regulatory background, and Mike Kansas, who has extensive experience in product development and testing to bring a product to U.S. Food and Drug Administration (FDA) approval. They subsequently added James Glenn, who has sales and marketing expertise. The core team forms the nucleus that can achieve several key milestones. As the milestones are met and surpassed, you start building out your infrastructure, which means hiring more people.

In building your core founding team, identify people who can multitask and are willing to take on lots of duties. Although someone with extensive experience can be a valuable addition, if that person has worked only in large corporations, it can be difficult for her to adjust to the start-up mentality. Corporate persons may expect all the administrative support they had at their previous companies. They may expect to focus narrowly on their areas of specialization. This can create a culture clash because in the start-up environment every team member needs to wear many hats. They all need to help others in areas that may not be their areas of expertise. They have to accomplish tasks with minimal administrative support (don't waste resources on administrative support too early in the launch phase). Although there are many other considerations in building a team, keeping the above advice in mind will help you launch your business and conserve resources.

Considering how important the team is to a company's success, you need to present the power of the team as effectively as possible. We suggest that you have an introductory paragraph that talks about how the team came together. The subsequent subsections will add detail about the team.

Team Bios and Roles

The best place to start is by identifying the founding team members and their titles. Often, the lead entrepreneur assumes a Chief Executive Officer (CEO) role. However, if you are young and have limited business experience, it is usually more productive to state that the company will seek a qualified CEO as it grows. In these cases, the lead entrepreneur may assume the role of chief technology officer (if she develops the technology) or that of vice president of business development. However, don't let these options confine you. The key is to convince investors that you have assembled the best team possible and that your team can execute the brilliant concept you are proposing.

Once responsibilities and titles have been defined, names and short bios should be filled in. The bios should demonstrate records of success. If you have started another business (even if it failed), highlight that company's accomplishments. If you have no previous entrepreneurial experience, discuss your achievements at your last job. For example, bios often contain a description of the number of people the entrepreneur previously managed and, more important, a measure of economic success, such as growing division sales by 20 percent or more. The bio should demonstrate your leadership capabilities. To complement this description, résumés often are included as an appendix.

Advisory Boards, Board of Directors, Strategic Partners, External Members

To enhance the team's credentials, many entrepreneurs find that they are more attractive to investors if they have strong advisory boards. In building an advisory board, identify individuals with relevant experience in your industry who can help you achieve important milestones. For example, FireFly has achieved several milestones (building a prototype, initial manufacturing run, initial sales) and has others that are targeted in the future. Child professionals have been critical to developing the product; thus, they are key advisers. Moving forward, FireFly needs to secure its distribution channels. Thus, it may seek advisers with contacts with institutions (hospitals, schools, philanthropic organizations) and specialty toy stores. Industry experts provide legitimacy to a new business as well as strong technical advice. Other advisory board members may bring other skills, such as financial, legal, or management expertise. Thus, it is common to see lawyers, professors, and accountants who can assist the venture's growth on advisory boards. Moreover, if your firm has a strategic supplier or key customer, it may make sense to invite that person onto the advisory board. Typically, these individuals are remunerated with a small equity stake and compensation for any organized meetings. The key in building the advisory board is to identify the key needs and milestones the organization will face during its launch phase.

By law, most organization types must have a board of directors. This is different from an advisory board, although board directors also can provide needed expertise. The primary role of the board of directors is to oversee the company on behalf of the investors. This fiduciary duty carries legal rights, obligations, and liabilities. As we have seen with the demise of large corporations such as Enron and Global Crossing, board directors may be sued if a corporation fails and shareholders believe the board members did not exert sufficient oversight of company officers. Sometimes a key industry expert will be willing to join the company as an advisor but not as a director because of liability issues but also because being a board director implies a long-term commitment to the company. Potential board members may not be interested in or willing to give the extra time that board directorship suggests. In any case, the business plan needs to describe the size of the board, its role in the organization, and any current board members. Most major investors, such as venture capitalists, will require one or more board seats. Usually the lead entrepreneur and one or more inside company members (e.g., chief financial officers, vice presidents) also will have board seats. At its current stage of development FireFly's board consists only of insiders. As it seeks and secures more equity infusions, investors probably will take board seats as well.

Strategic partners may not necessarily be on your advisory board or board of directors but still provide credibility to your venture. In such cases it makes sense to highlight their involvement in the company's success. It is also common to list external team members, such as the law firm and the accounting firm your venture uses. The key in this section is to demonstrate that your firm can execute the concept successfully. A strong team provides the foundation that conveys the idea that your venture will implement the opportunity successfully.

Compensation and Ownership

A capstone to the team section should be a table containing key team members by role, compensation, and ownership equity. A brief description of the table should explain why the compensation is appropriate. Many entrepreneurs choose not to pay themselves in the early months. Although this strategy conserves cash flow, it misrepresents the individual's worth to the organization. Therefore, the table should contain the salary the employee is due, and then, if deemed necessary, that salary can be deferred until a time when cash flow is strong. Another column that can be powerful shows what the person's current or most recent compensation was and what he will be paid in the new company. We are most impressed when we see highly qualified entrepreneurs taking a smaller salary than they earned at their previous jobs. It suggests that an entrepreneur really believes in the upside payoff the company's growth will generate. Of course, the entrepreneur plans to increase this salary as the venture grows and starts to thrive. Thus, the description of the schedule should underscore the plan to increase salaries in the future. It is also a good idea to hold stock aside for future key hires and establish a stock option pool for lower-level but critical employees, such as software engineers. It is not uncommon to see a management set-aside of 15 percent of the company. Again, the plan should discuss such provisions.

FireFly Management Team Plan

8.0 MANAGEMENT TEAM

FireFly is the brainchild of Lauren McLaughlin, building on her passion for kids. Currently the Company consists of Lauren and a part-time director of marketing. Upon closing the next round of financing, the Company will build out its infrastructure.

> Note that this company is still in the early stages of launch. It is common to have several of the team members working part-time, especially since it preserves cash. However, having only one fully committed player may cause investors concern. They may question whether Lauren can build the team necessary to succeed.

CEO/Founder: Lauren McLaughlin has 10 years of experience working with children in difficult life situations as a teacher, counselor, and program manager. She graduated with an MBA from the F.W. Olin College of Business at Babson College. Lauren designed teaching curricula for Sunburst Projects, a cutting-edge nonprofit serving children with AIDS. She also worked for the YWCA, revitalizing the Teen Women Entrepreneurs Program, an entrepreneurship program for at-risk youth. Lauren's experience, combined with her business education and background, makes her well suited to lead the company.

Director of Marketing: Megan MacDonald's previous roles include a marketing internship at Hasbro, Inc., the world's second largest toy manufacturer. While there she assisted in the launch and development of girls' and creative play products. She held client management and market research positions at Forrester Research, Inc., and was a marketing assistant with Junior Achievement of Greater Puget Sound. Megan received her bachelor of arts degree in English and Spanish from Colby College and graduated magna cum laude from the F.W. Olin Graduate School of Business at Babson College with a concentration in marketing.

8.1 Board of Advisers

FireFly has developed a board of advisers to offer guidance on toy design, distribution, and business acumen. The advisers will provide their expertise both through counsel and through contributing to the guides for caregivers.

Dr. Julie Riess: Received her A.B. from Vassar College and her Ph.D. in developmental and social psychology from Brandeis University. Trained as a developmental psychologist and elementary education teacher, she has focused on linking developmental theory and basic research with educational and parenting practices. She also serves as a consultant for early child-care facilities and lectures on topics focusing on improving the quality of child care for all children. Recently, she codesigned an infant-toddler exhibit for the Mid-Hudson Children's Museum. She currently serves as chair of the board of the Dutchess County Child Development Council and as a board member of the Mid-Hudson Children's Museum.

Richard Cook:[1] Executive director of the Winston child care center, Cook has been a member of the faculty at Boston City University while leading the early childhood teacher preparation program. During the 1980s he served as vice chair of the advisory council on early care and the education of young

---

[1] Richard Cook and Lisa Andrews are disguised names, as are their professional affiliations.

children for the Massachusetts Board of Education. He has been a research associate at the Moon Center for Mental Retardation and the Family and Children's Policy Center at Boston City University. His awards have included a National Institute of Health Training Fellowship for the study of public policy and supports for people with special needs.

Lisa Andrews:[1] Lisa is a head preschool teacher at the Winston child care center. She is a recent graduate of Vassar College, where she worked for several years at the Wimpfheimer Nursery School. Lisa uses creative movement and handmade felt figures to make stories come alive for the children. She provides the insight into caregiver needs and concerns.

Dr. Andrew "Zach" Zacharakis: Professor Zacharakis is the Paul T. Babson term chair in entrepreneurship at the Arthur M. Blank Center for Entrepreneurship, Babson College. Prior to entering academia, Zach was with Leisure Technology, IBM, and The Cambridge Companies (a venture capital firm). He brings years of experience working with entrepreneurs and investors.

8.2 Ownership and Compensation

> Although the team is small, Lauren might consider adding a table describing her compensation in detail.

Currently, Lauren McLaughlin, the founder and CEO, owns 95% of the company, with 5% owned by initial investors. At present, all compensation is deferred as Lauren and Megan focus on launching the business. Once the next round of financing is secured, the Company will begin to pay salaries.

Chapter Summary

The team section is critical to selling your vision successfully. You need to build a team that adds credibility. This may be difficult for younger entrepreneurs and those who are entering a field where they have little experience. If you find that your team section isn't compelling, you probably need to add a key member or two. Your ability to build a strong team is your first market test. If you can convince others of the attractiveness of the opportunity, you've passed a major milestone that will make your company more attractive to investors and other stakeholders.

9

THE CRITICAL RISKS AND OFFERING PLAN SECTIONS

Critical Risks: Understanding the Critical Drivers of Your Success

Every new venture faces a number of risks that may threaten its survival. Although the business plan has been creating a story of success, there are a number of threats that readers will identify and recognize. The plan needs to acknowledge these potential risks; otherwise investors will believe that the entrepreneur is naive or untrustworthy and may withhold investment. It is also important for you to understand these critical risks because they most often are directly related to assumptions that will drive your venture's success or failure. For example, a common critical risk is market acceptance. Will your target customers buy your product in the quantity and price you expect? If they do, your top-line revenue projections probably will hold true, but if they do not, your business could be in serious trouble. How should you present these critical risks without scaring your investors or, for that matter, so that you feel comfortable proceeding with the venture? Identify the risk and then state your contingency plan. For instance, if your primary target customer doesn't buy your product as expected, a contingency might be to redirect your efforts toward a new customer group. Critical assumptions vary from one company to another, but some common categories are market interest and growth potential, competitor actions and retaliation, time and cost of development, operating expenses, and availability and timing of financing. We will highlight these major categories briefly, but don't limit your thinking to these categories. Try to anticipate what else may be important for your company.

Market Interest and Growth Potential

The biggest risk any new venture faces is that once the product is developed, no one will buy it. Although a number of things can be done to minimize this risk, such as market research, focus groups, and beta sites, it is difficult to gauge overall demand and growth of that demand until your product hits the market. This risk must be stated but countered with the tactics and contingencies the company will undertake if problems develop. For example, sales risk can be reduced by instituting an effective advertising and marketing plan or by identifying not only a primary target customer but also secondary and tertiary target customers that the company will seek if the primary customer proves not to be interested.

Perhaps the most effective method of countering this risk is to test the market in a series of iterations. Thus, many technology companies go through alpha and beta testing. Basically, alpha testing involves having your employees and friends test the product. They report back, and you make modifications so that the product better meets their needs. Next, you might move the product to beta sites. A beta site is a handful of selected customers who understand that the product is in an early stage and that there may be glitches yet are excited by the product's potential. Usually you can get these customers to pay a minimal price for the product, but sometimes you let them use it for free. After you make adjustments during the beta stage, you start a controlled rollout to the broader market. Try to have feedback loops where you can learn from the customers and make changes so that the product is better in the next version. Although this strategy is associated with technology products such as software, it can work with all businesses.

FireFly, for example, produced a prototype of its first Comfort Creature and then distributed it to a few child-care professionals. Lauren then observed the professionals and children playing with the toy and, based on feedback, made adjustments. In the next phase Lauren donated a few toys to a charitable event and followed up with the people who used the product to make it better. She also sold a few toys to friends and close advisers (including one of the authors) and asked them to provide feedback on how their children used the product. At the time when this current business plan is written, FireFly has done only a limited run of 500 Comfort Creatures and Comfort Kits. Based on the reaction from selling this first production run, Lauren will make adjustments before producing a larger run. The key is to have several iterations where you can test and then adjust the product offering so that it better meets the customer's needs. This strategy minimizes the risk of misreading the customer. You'll also note that you have reduced resource outlays by using a controlled strategy. The cost of producing 500 Comfort Creatures is lower than that of a larger production run, and if customers don't like the product, you will have saved the difference in cost between a smaller and a larger production batch. Often this can be the difference between surviving and failing. If you blow all your resources on a large production run that fails, you may not get a second chance. In contrast, conserving your resources on a smaller test run should preserve enough resources to make changes and try again.

Competitors' Actions and Retaliation

Having had the opportunity to work with entrepreneurs and student entrepreneurs over the years, we have been struck by the firmly held belief either that direct competition didn't exist or that it was sleepy and slow to react. There have been many cases where this indeed has been true, but we caution against using it as a key assumption in your venture's success. Most entrepreneurs passionately believe that they are offering something new and wonderful that is clearly different from what is being offered currently. They go on to state that the existing competition won't attack their niche in the near future, often because the competition is a large company concerned only with the larger market. The implicit assumption is that your smaller niche isn't interesting to the competition because the potential profitability of the niche is lower than that of the broader market. The risk that this assessment is wrong should be acknowledged. One counter to this threat is that your venture has room in its gross margins and cash available to withstand and fight back against such attacks. You also should identify some strategies to protect and reposition yourself if an attack occurs.

Time and Cost to Development

As was mentioned in the development plan section, many factors can delay and add to the expense of developing your product. The business plan should identify the factors that may hinder development. For instance, during the extended high-tech boom of the late 1990s, there was an acute shortage of skilled software engineers. That led to the risk of hiring and retaining the most qualified professionals. One way to counter the problem might be to outsource some development to underemployed engineers in India. Compensation, equity participation, flexible hours, and other benefits the firm could offer also might minimize the risk.

Operating Expenses

Operating expenses have a way of growing beyond expectations. Sales and administration, marketing, and interest expenses are some of the areas an entrepreneur needs to monitor and manage. The business plan should highlight how these expenses were forecast (comparable companies and detailed analysis) but also talk about contingencies such as slowing the hiring of support personnel, especially if development or other key tasks take longer than expected.

Availability and Timing of Financing

We can't stress enough how important cash flow is to the survival and flourishing of a new venture. One major risk that most new ventures face is that they will have difficulty obtaining needed financing, both equity and debt. If the current business plan is meant to attract investors and is successful, that isn't a near-term risk, but most ventures will need follow-on financing. If the firm fails to make progress (or meet key milestones), it may not be able to secure additional financing on favorable terms. A counter to this risk is to identify alternative sources that are viable or strategies to slow the "burn rate."[1]

A number of other risks might apply to your business. Acknowledge them and discuss how you can overcome them. Doing so generates confidence in your investors.

---

[1] The burn rate is how much more cash the company is expending each month than it is earning in revenue.

FireFly Critical Risk Section

9.0 CRITICAL RISKS

9.1 Market Interest and Growth Potential

> Risk.

The product is not sufficiently differentiated from a teddy bear product in the eyes of the caregivers. FireFly's product line includes plush animals, kits with special stories and activities addressing different life challenges, and guides for caregivers who are helping children manage these challenges. The Company believes this differentiates our product from teddy bears. FireFly also recognizes that caregivers respond best to touching and experiencing new products and enjoy finding new tools to take into the classroom and offer to parents. FireFly will work with caregivers through the website and sales force and at conferences to educate them on how to use Comfort Creatures creatively. These demonstrations will clarify the products' uniqueness.

> Response. Additional features that the market should value as well as special communication to reach the market.

9.2 Distribution

> Risk.

Unique distribution channels will not prove successful. The therapeutic toys FireFly makes are well suited to unique distribution through philanthropic organizations, hospitals, and schools. The Company has tested the concept through its advisers and discussions with various organizations. Feedback suggests that these channels are interested and willing to deliver FireFly's unique tools to caregivers. In case these channels don't prove out, the Company also is developing the specialty toy store channel.

> Response. Tested channel and is developing an alternative channel.

9.3 Time and Cost to Development

> Risk.

There are risks to outsourcing manufacturing. Since the control of the manufacturing is ultimately not within the company's control, it is an inherent risk. The initial production of 500 Comfort Creatures and Comfort Kits suggests that the Company has found a reliable partner in The Five of Us. FireFly also is developing contingency relationships in case unforeseen problems arise.

> Response. Initial manufacturing run has been successful and FireFly is identifying alternative sources.

9.4 Intellectual Property

> Risk.

Competitors could mimic our product. The products will be protected through trademarks and copyrights. The concept and story line for the creatures and the guidelines for the caregivers will be protected by copyright.

> Response. Using legal protections as much as possible.

Critical Risks Summary

As you review FireFly's critical risks section, note that Lauren raises the risk and then discusses how the company is managing it. What other risks do you think Lauren has overlooked? Do you believe she has countered those risks adequately? What other contingencies might improve her chances of success if some of these risks come into play? The key is to anticipate what might happen and prepare to manage those risks if they arise.

Offering Plan: How Much Do You Need?

As we stated in Chapter 1, one of the main reasons to write a business plan is to seek and secure financing. It is important for entrepreneurs to identify not only how much capital they are seeking but also how they will use that funding to achieve milestones. A "sources and uses" table articulates your needs effectively. The sources section details how much capital the entrepreneur needs and the types of financing, such as equity investment and debt infusions. The uses section details how the money will be spent. Typically, the entrepreneur should secure enough financing to last 12 to 18 months. Taking more capital means that the entrepreneur gives up more equity. In other words, taking more capital than you need dilutes your ownership share. Taking less means that the entrepreneur may run out of cash before reaching milestones that equate to higher valuations.

It is important to think of financing as happening over time. You want to raise enough capital during each stage to reach a critical milestone and then raise additional capital to hit the next milestone. This financing strategy preserves your equity because you give up equity based on the perceived value of the company at the time of financing. When you are starting out, you may have only a concept, not a product. The value of that concept (and therefore of the company) is relatively lower than the value will be when you have a physical product that is a manifestation of the concept. Likewise, a company that has a physical product but few or no sales is valued less than is a company that has sales. If at the time you start your company you have raised all the capital you need to penetrate the market and reach a certain sales level (cash flow positive), you probably will have to give away most of the equity because the value of the company is so low in the beginning. In contrast, if you manage the financing over time, you will give up less equity in total.

A question that most entrepreneurs have difficulty answering is how much of the company they must give to investors at each stage of financing, or what the company's valuation is. The reality is that valuation is always a matter of negotiation between you and your investors. With that understanding, a company's valuation is based on what it has accomplished to date, or, said differently, what milestones it has achieved. A company that is prelaunch (just a concept) is worth very little. Developing a product increases the value. Achieving sales increases the value further. So how might you gauge the value of your company at this stage? One technique that is relatively simple and robust is the venture capital technique. Don't worry; you don't need to be seeking venture capital to use it.

The technique basically looks at what return an investor needs to achieve and then looks at the company's potential to generate that return. For example, we see from FireFly's business plan that the company is seeking $320,000. Since the company has a product and limited sales, investors will gauge the likelihood that they will get their investment back plus an attractive rate of return. The rate of return an investor might expect would be around 50 percent per year. Why? The chances are still great that the venture will fail, and so investors need a premium return or they will invest elsewhere. When an investor puts money into a start-up firm, that firm is privately held. That means there is no market for investors to sell their shares. Thus, investors expect to hold their shares for many years until the company (1) goes public, (2) is acquired by another firm (for example, American Girl was acquired by Mattel), or (3) generates enough cash flow and profit to buy back the investors' shares. Let's assume that investors expect to get their money out of the company in five years. That means that

Investment (i) = $320,000
Length of investment (n) = 5 years
Expected rate of return (ROR) = 50%
We are seeking the future value of the investment (FV)

$FV = i(1 + ROR)^n$
$FV = \$320,000 \ (1 + .50)^5$
$FV = \$2,430,000$

Now that we know the future value of the investment, we need to determine the future value of the company. We need to estimate the company's profit after tax in the future and then multiply that figure by a price-earnings ratio. In this case, I'm using the projections that FireFly presents in its plan for year 5.

FireFly's profit after tax (PAT) = $4.6million
Consumer durables price-earnings ratio (PE)[2] = 15
FV = PAT * PE
FV = $4.6M * 15
FV = $69M

The final step is to divide the FV of the investment by the FV of the company. What we are basically doing is determining what percentage of the company the investors need to own so that they can earn their expected rate of return.

$$\$2.4M/\$69M = 3.5\%$$

As investors, we are always skeptical about an entrepreneur's projections. Entrepreneurs tend to be overly optimistic. Thus, you need to be careful when going through this exercise so that you will not be surprised if an investor has a significantly different estimate. There are several assumptions that can be widely off. Based on our extensive experience, for instance, we would demand 20 percent of FireFly's equity. That percentage suggests that FireFly is worth roughly $1.5 million before the investment (divide $320,000 by 20 percent). We are in essence questioning the accuracy of Lauren's financial projections. As we discussed in earlier chapters, we believe she is underestimating her employee expenses. Thus, we expect her to have higher operating expenses, which equates to lower profits and a lower valuation over time.

Even though we recommend that you have some basis for determining how much equity you need to give to secure investment, we do not suggest that you present that in the business plan. This gets back to our opening statement that valuation is a negotiation. Thus, putting in how

---

[2]From *Business Week* 2002 3rd Quarter Corporate Scorecard, http://bwnt.business-week.com/corp_profits/2002/q3_index.asp?industry=2.

much you are willing to give might end the negotiation before it starts. If, for instance, we saw that FireFly wants to relinquish only 3.4 percent of its equity for my $320,000, we probably would not consider the investment. Nonetheless, it is important to go through this exercise so that you are operating from a position of knowledge when you negotiate with investors. Thus, the offering section is often very short, possibly consisting of only a sources and uses table with some description around it.

FireFly Offering Plan

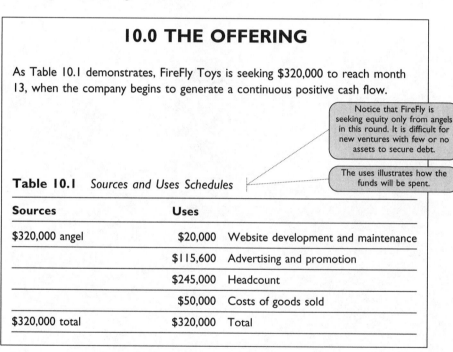

10.0 THE OFFERING

As Table 10.1 demonstrates, FireFly Toys is seeking $320,000 to reach month 13, when the company begins to generate a continuous positive cash flow.

> Notice that FireFly is seeking equity only from angels in this round. It is difficult for new ventures with few or no assets to secure debt.

> The uses illustrates how the funds will be spent.

Table 10.1   *Sources and Uses Schedules*

Sources	Uses	
$320,000 angel		
	$20,000	Website development and maintenance
	$115,600	Advertising and promotion
	$245,000	Headcount
	$50,000	Costs of goods sold
$320,000 total	$320,000	Total

Chapter Summary

In this chapter we have focused on the critical assumptions that drive a venture's success and also the offering plan. Both elements are influenced by your pro forma projections. Your critical assumptions often are directly related to the revenue and cost projections that we will see on your income statement. Your offering valuation also is derived from your income statement projections. Chapter 10 will examine how to develop sound financial projections.

10 FINANCIAL PLAN: TELLING YOUR STORY IN NUMBERS

If the proceeding plan is your verbal description of the opportunity and the way you will execute it, the financial plan is the mathematical equivalent. The growth in revenues speaks to the upside of your opportunity. The expenses indicate how much it costs to deliver the product or service. Cash flow statements serve as an early warning system for potential problems (or critical risks), and the balance sheet represents the resources required to put the delivery system in place. That said, generating realistic financials is one of the most intimidating hurdles many entrepreneurs face. There is a temptation to hire an accountant to create your financials for you. That's a big mistake. Although the process is painful, the deep learning you acquire by struggling through the numbers helps you understand the business. Always remember that the numbers in the financial statements are a reflection of the actions you take in your business. You learn what actions drive revenue and costs. You learn how cash flow can go negative even if you are growing and profitable. Besides, you will be presenting your plan to investors and bankers. You will lose credibility if you can't explain the numbers.

This chapter will provide you with a broad overview of how to generate realistic financials. We will highlight a dual approach to building your model: comparable analysis and the build-up technique. Entrepreneurs should use both approaches, and with work and skill, the two approaches will allow an entrepreneur to paint a textured picture of the financial structure of the new venture.

Creating Initial Estimates
Comparable Method

Entrepreneurs are notoriously optimistic in their projections. One term entrepreneurs overuse in the business plan, especially the financial plan, is *conservative estimate*. History proves that 99 percent of all entrepreneurs are amazingly aggressive in their projections. Professional investors recognize this problem and often discount financials up to 50 percent from the entrepreneur's projections. That action greatly affects the valuation of your company and means you will have to give up more equity for the needed financing. How do you prevent this unhappy surprise from happening? Validate your projections by comparing your firm's pro forma financials with existing firms' actual performance. If you can convince investors that your projections are reasonable and refer to existing companies as a basis for your beliefs, you will get a valuation closer to what you expected. Obviously, no two firms are exactly alike, and if you were to launch an online bookstore, it would be unlikely that your firm would mirror Amazon.com perfectly. However, the comparable method doesn't mean that you substitute another firm's financials for your own; it means that you use that as a starting point. Early in this process variances will emerge that require analysis and explanation. Some of the variances will highlight your competitive advantages; others will be red flags marking weaknesses. Many of the variances may be explained by the stage of your company's development. New ventures go through a learning process that translates into less efficient use of resources early on (higher expenses). You need to understand why the differences exist.

The first step is to start with your benchmark company's common-sized income statement through the use of percentages for all line items. With the revenue line equaling 100 percent, work your way down the income statement and express each line (cost of goods sold, gross margin, etc.) as a percentage of revenue. The Vermont Teddy Bear Company (VTBC) is a good comparable. Exhibit 10.1 shows FireFly and VTBC

Exhibit 10.1 *Common-Sized Income Sheet Comparison*

	FireFly 2007		Vermont Teddy Bear 2001		Variance
REVENUES	24.2	100%	37.3	100%	0%
COST OF REVENUE	6.4	26%	13.4	36%	−9%
GROSS PROFIT	17.8	74%	23.9	64%	9%
Sales and marketing	7.6	31%	14.8	40%	−8%
Product development	0.4	2%		0%	2%
General and administration	2.2	9%	4.7	13%	−4%
Total operating expenses	10.2	42%	19.5	52%	−10%
Earnings before interest and taxes	7.6	31%	4.4	12%	20%
Interest income	0.0	0%	(0.3)	−1%	1%
Net earnings before taxes	7.6	31%	4.2	11%	20%
Taxes	(3.0)	−12%	1.6	4%	−17%
Net income	4.6	19%	2.6	7%	12%

side by side. We can see that FireFly's gross margin is 9 percent higher than VTBC's. This may be explainable by the higher production costs of VTBC. VTBC operates its own production factory in the United States versus outsourcing to cheaper factories in Asia. An area of bigger concern is that FireFly's operating expenses are 10 percent lower than those of VTBC. This suggests that FireFly may be underestimating the costs of generating its sales. If you recall our discussion in Chapter 6 of the amount of sales per employee, it appears that FireFly will need to build a larger infrastructure to meet its sales goals. Remember, gross variance, positive or negative, from the comparable companies will draw investors' attention and *should* draw your attention. If you understand these discrepancies, you can address investors' concerns with confidence, increasing your credibility.

If we were potential investors in FireFly, we would question its labor projections. If Lauren couldn't explain her lower sales and marketing expenses satisfactorily, we would be hesitant to invest. VTBC relies primarily on direct distribution, and so Lauren might be able to argue that its marketing and sales infrastructure should be greater. However, that higher expense probably would be offset by gaining higher gross margins (VTBC gets the retail price through its direct channels). Even considering FireFly's unique distribution strategy, we think she underestimates how many sales reps she will need to support those channels.

Individual company benchmarks are a good foundation to build on, but we also would look at industry averages. The *Almanac of Business and Industrial Financial Ratios* and *Industry Norms and Key Business Ratios* published by Dun and Bradstreet are excellent sources to use as starting points in building financial statements relevant to your industry. Secondary sources also break down industries by firm size. For example, smaller firms have common-sized percentages different from those of larger firms. Thus, these sources help entrepreneurs build income statements by providing industry averages for costs of goods sold, salary expenses, interest expenses, and so on. Again, your firm will differ from these industry averages, but you should be able to explain why it differs.

Build-Up Method

The second method is the build-up method. This approach derives from the scientific finding that people make better decisions by decomposing a problem into smaller parts. For financial pro forma construction this is relatively easy. The place to start is the income statement. Identify all your revenue sources (usually the various product offerings). Instead of visualizing what you will sell in a month or a year, break it down to the day. For example, if you are starting a new restaurant, you should estimate how many customers you might serve in a particular day and how much they would spend per visit based on the types of meals and beverages they would buy. In essence, you are developing an average ticket price per customer. Then multiply that by the number of days of operation in the year. Once you have the typical day, you can make adjustments to take account of cyclical aspects of the business such as slow days or slow months. You then could multiply your estimates if you were to open up a chain of restaurants. Once you have gone through a couple of iterations of each approach, you should be able to reconcile the differences.

One schedule that is particularly powerful in building up cost estimates is a headcount schedule. In Chapter 7 we saw the headcount table for FireFly. Next, assign average salaries to these employees and then funnel the salaries into the appropriate income statement lines. We also must remember that employees cost more than just their salaries and wages. You will have to pay employment taxes (Social Security, etc.) and possibly health insurance and any other benefits you wish to provide. This is sometimes called the *labor burden,* and we multiply salary by a burden rate. Fifteen percent is usually a good first estimate. Breaking down to this level of detail enables entrepreneurs to be more accurate in aggregating up to their real headcount expenses, which tend to be the major line item in most companies.

The Financial Statements

Going through these exercises allows you to construct a "realistic" set of pro forma financials. The financial statements that must be included in your plan are the income statement, the cash flow statement, and the balance sheet. Investors typically expect five years of financials, recognizing that the farther out one goes, the less accurate the forecasts are. The rationale behind five years is that the first two years show the firm surviving and the last three show the upside growth potential. The majority of new ventures lose money for the first two years. Therefore, the income statement and cash flow statement should be month to month during the first two years to show how much cash is needed until the firm can become self-sustaining. Month-to-month analysis shows cash flow decreasing and provides an early warning for when the entrepreneur should seek the next round of financing. Years 3 through 5 need to be illustrated only on an annual basis as this communicates your vision for growth and a textured understanding of the forces you believe will drive the future of the business. The balance sheet can be on an annual basis for all five years since it is presenting a snapshot on the last day of a particular period, but it will inform the investors of the magnitude of the resources you expect to marshal to fulfill your vision.

The key to constructing the actual financials is building the statements on a spreadsheet and linking the different financials statements together. This can be difficult, but Frank Moyes and Steve Lawrence at the University of Colorado have developed an excellent Excel template that you can download from their website.[1]

---

[1]http://leeds.colorado.edu/bplan/html/spTools.html. Hit the financials hotlink.

Description of Statements

Once the financial spreadsheets are complete, a two- to three-page explanation of the financials should be written and should precede the statements. Although you understand all the assumptions and comparables that went into building the financial forecast, the reader needs to have the background spelled out. The explanation should have four subheadings: overview, income statement, cash flow, and balance sheet. The overview section should highlight the major assumptions that drive your revenue and expenses. This section should map several of the critical risks you identified earlier. The income statement description goes into more detail about some of the revenue and cost drivers that haven't been discussed in the overview section. The cash flow description talks about the timing of cash infusions, accounts payable, accounts receivable, and so forth. The balance sheet description illustrates how major ratios change as the firm grows. For instance, talk about the inventory turn ratio. How long do you hold inventory before it is sold? This has a major impact on the company's cash position because holding inventory means that cash is tied up.

FireFly Financial Plan

11.0 THE FINANCIAL PLAN

FireFly generates revenue by selling Comfort Creatures and Comfort Kits through three primary distribution channels: institutions, specialty retail, and

> Articulates primary revenue drivers.

direct sales. Institutional channels constitute the majority of sales (starting at 85% and falling to 66%). Wholesale to specialty toy stores will be the next most important channel, and direct sales through the website are expected to account for only 5% of all sales. After closing the next round of financing, FireFly will ramp up its operations by expanding its efforts in these channels aggressively.

> Summarizes FireFly's limited operating history. This communicates that the company has tested its business model and is ready to ramp it up.

11.1 Actuals

FireFly has been operating since September 2002. During this initial phase, we have proved production and the salability of our products (Exhibit 11.1). To date, the Company has sold 126 Comfort Creatures and 75 Comfort kits, totaling almost $10,000 in revenue. Upon closing the current round of financing, FireFly will scale up production and sales. The financial pro forma projections suggest that the business model has high potential.

Visuals draw the reader in.

Exhibit 11.1 *Total Sales through December 2002*

	Sept.	**Oct.**	**Nov.**	**Dec.**
Jordos				
Units	40	60	10	16
Sales	$1,600	$2,400	$400	$640
Kits				
	40	20	5	10
	$2,600	$1,300	$325	$650
Total	$4,240	$3,720	$730	$1,300
Total cumulative sales				$9,990

11.2 Income Statement

Sales are driven by product lines, channel penetration, and geographic expansion. In year 1 FireFly will focus primarily on philanthropic organizations (institutions) and specialty retail toy stores in New England and New York. Toward the middle of year 1 the second Comfort Creature (Mooshi) and Comfort Kit (Divorce) will be introduced. In year 2 the Company will expand to Chicago and San Francisco as well as continue to develop new Creatures and Kits. In years 3 through 5 FireFly will continue its nationwide expansion and add new product introductions. Exhibit 11.2 shows the revenue projections by distribution channel for the next 5 years.

Offers more details on revenue drivers. This allows the reader to judge whether the revenue forecasts are reasonable.

Exhibit 11.2 *Revenue Projections*

Detailed revenue forecasts by distribution channel and product category help reader gauge reasonableness of projection.

Years 1 to 5	2003	2004	2005	2006	2007
Institutional sales					
Comfort Creatures					
Number of units	14,365	53,460	108,570	202,455	304,343
Price per unit	32	32	32	32	32
Total	$459,680	$1,710,720	$3,474,240	$6,478,560	$9,738,960

Notice that unit sales explode from 14,000 units in 2003 to over 300,000 units in year 5. Lauren would argue that the growth is a function of new product introductions, additional channels, and geographic expansion. Make sure you understand what drives your sales growth.

(continues)

Exhibit 11.2 *continued*

Years I to 5	2003	2004	2005	2006	2007
Comfort Kits					
Number of units	4,250	26,400	52,800	83,490	142,230
Price per unit	52	52	52	52	52
Total	$221,000	$1,372,800	$2,745,600	$4,341,480	$7,395,960
Total Institutional	$680,680	$3,083,520	$6,219,840	$10,820,040	$17,134,920
Wholesale sales					
Comfort Creatures					
Number of units	1,690	23,490	47,705	88,958	133,726
Price per unit	20	20	20	20	20
Total	$33,800	$469,800	$954,100	$1,779,150	$2,674,525
Comfort Kits					
Number of units	500	11,600	23,200	36,685	62,495
Price per unit	45	45	45	45	45
Total	$22,500	$522,000	$1,044,000	$1,650,825	$2,812,275
Total Wholesale	$56,300	$991,800	$1,998,100	$3,429,975	$5,486,800
Direct sales					
Comfort Creatures					
Number of units	845	4,050	8,225	15,338	23,056
Price per unit	40	40	40	40	40
Total	$33,800	$162,000	$329,000	$613,500	$922,250
Comfort Kits					
Number of units	250	2,000	4,000	6,325	10,775
Price per unit	65	65	65	65	65
Total	$16,250	$130,000	$260,000	$411,125	$700,375
Total direct	$50,050	$292,000	$589,000	$1,024,625	$1,622,625
Total revenue	$787,030	$4,367,320	$8,806,940	$15,274,640	$24,244,345

> Attempting to validate high gross margins because FireFly expects potential investors to question them. It is always wise to validate major assumptions as well as possible.

Gross margins vary by product and channel (see Exhibit 11.3). Gross margins are significantly higher than the industry average due to premium pricing and unique distribution channels. Cost of goods sold (COGS) is higher in year 1 than in subsequent years due to minimum charges on shipping goods from China and minimum charges on fulfillment from our warehouse vendor. After we achieve some scale, the overall COGS drops dramatically.

> It is typical for new firms to have high operating costs initially. Companies typically need to incur expenses before they generate revenues. New employees and their associated salaries are often the major expense.

In the first year the operating costs are 79% of total revenue. Legal fees, salaries, promotion, and advertising will account for the bulk of the costs in the first year. The construction and maintenance of the e-commerce website will be the largest promotional expense. By the second year the company will still be focused on increasing promotion and adding members of the management team. The experiences in the first year and the additional people on staff will increase the operational efficiencies of the company. By the second year operating costs will be down to 44% of revenues. Exhibit 11.4 shows the income statement for the first 5 years.

Exhibit 11.3   *Gross Margins by Channel*

	Institution	Wholesale	Direct
Comfort Creature			
Price/unit	$32	$20	$40
COGS	$9	$9	$9
GM	$23	$11	$31
%	72%	55%	78%
Comfort Kits			
Price/unit	$52	$45	$65
COGS	$26	$26	$26
GM	$26	$19	$39
%	50%	42%	60%

> Notice the level of detail of expenses. Coupled with the detailed revenue model in Exhibit 11.2, this gives the potential reader a sense of your business model. It also helps you understand the levers you can pull to conserve cash. For instance, FireFly can defer salaries if cash flow becomes strained.

Exhibit 11.4   *Income Statement Years 1 to 5 ($)*

	2003	2004	2005	2006	2007
REVENUES	787,030	4,367,320	8,806,940	15,274,640	24,244,345
COST OF REVENUE	367,949	1,295,373	2,368,554	4,159,758	6,447,854
% of revenues	47%	30%	27%	27%	27%
GROSS PROFIT	419,081	3,071,947	6,438,387	11,114,883	17,796,491
% of revenues	53%	70%	73%	73%	73%
Sales and Marketing					
Salaries and benefits	30,000	395,750	1,237,300	2,302,000	4,362,500
Target bonus as percent of salary	9,900	130,598	408,309	759,660	1,439,625
Recruiting cost			123,730	230,200	436,250
Samples	2,840	3,408	4,090	4,908	5,889
Conference fees/booth	21,100	31,650	47,475	71,213	71,213
Materials	48,000	100,000	150,000	225,000	337,500
Website creation	20,000	4,000	8,000	16,000	16,000
Website maintenance	24,000	24,000	24,000	24,000	24,000
Direct mailings	0	40,000	40,000	60,000	80,000
Advertising and public relations	115,600	150,000	200,000	250,000	300,000
All other expenses % of revenue	78,703	436,732	176,139	305,493	484,887
Total Sales and Marketing	350,143	1,316,138	2,419,042	4,248,473	7,557,863

(continues)

Exhibit 11.4 *continued*

	2003	2004	2005	2006	2007
Product Development					
Salaries and benefits	0	0	81,900	120,000	144,000
Graphic design/illustration	35,000	40,000	80,000	80,000	160,000
Writing/editing	20,000	25,000	28,000	28,000	60,000
Other fees	4,000	8,000	8,000	8,000	8,000
Total Product Development	59,000	73,000	197,900	236,000	372,000
General and Administration					
Salaries and benefits	90,000	218,000	264,650	308,000	1,380,000
Depreciation	(3,667)	(13,667)	(25,000)	(46,667)	(70,000)
Rent and utilities	5,000	50,000	80,000	100,000	100,000
Product liability insurance	6,900	8,900	8,900	8,900	8,900
Legal fees	12,000	18,000	25,000	35,000	35,000
Capital expenditures	11,000	30,000	45,000	65,000	100,000
Accounting fees	10,000				
All other expenses % of revenue	78,703	218,366	440,347	763,732	727,330
Total General and Administration	209,936	529,599	838,897	1,233,965	2,281,230
Total Operating Expenses	619,079	1,918,737	3,455,839	5,718,438	10,211,094
% of revenue	78.7%	43.9%	39.2%	37.4%	42.1%
Earnings before Interest and Taxes	(199,999)	1,153,210	2,982,547	5,396,444	7,585,397
Interest Income	0	(18,000)	0	0	10,000
Net Earnings before Taxes	(199,999)	1,135,210	2,982,547	5,396,444	7,595,397
Taxes	0	(374,084)	(1,193,019)	(2,158,578)	(3,038,159)
Net Income	(199,999)	761,126	1,789,528	3,237,867	4,557,238
% of Revenue	−25%	17%	20%	21%	19%

> It is important to show monthly statements in the early years to illustrate seasonality and other factors that might be hidden in yearly statements.

Exhibit 11.5 shows the income statements on a monthly basis for the first 2 years. Revenue and expenses ramp up in year 1 as the Company enters the institution and specialty retail store channels. FireFly sales and marketing expenses are higher in January 2003 as the Company initiates its efforts. Sales drop off in January 2004 due to the postholiday decline, although FireFly is less cyclical than other toy manufacturers due to the nature of the product and distribution channel.

FireFly doesn't show much seasonality. There is a ramp-up around December, but the drop-off to year 2 January is less than we would expect even though its primary distribution channel is institutions.

Exhibit 11.5 FireFly Toys Income Statements Year 1 by Months ($)

	Jan.	Feb.	Mar.	Apr.	May	June	July	Aug.	Sept.	Oct.	Nov.	Dec.	12 Months
NET REVENUES	520	1,559	1,819	4,938	10,133	41,590	47,830	67,595	88,375	145,550	161,150	215,972	787,030
COST OF REVENUE	243	729	850	2,308	4,737	19,444	22,361	31,602	41,317	68,047	75,340	100,971	367,949
GROSS PROFIT	277	830	969	2,629	5,395	22,146	25,469	35,993	47,058	77,503	85,810	115,002	419,081
OPERATING EXPENSES													
Sales and marketing	22,040	18,100	12,100	19,000	18,300	15,899	40,217	36,617	35,617	45,617	45,617	41,018	350,143
Product development + A2I	4,917	4,917	4,917	4,917	4,917	4,917	4,917	4,917	4,917	4,917	4,917	4,917	59,000
General and administration	8,325	4,325	4,325	16,075	9,325	9,325	25,192	26,442	25,192	22,442	25,192	33,776	209,936
Total operating expenses	35,282	27,342	21,342	39,992	32,542	30,141	70,326	67,976	65,726	72,976	75,726	79,710	619,079
EARNINGS FROM OPERATIONS	(35,005)	(26,511)	(20,373)	(37,363)	(27,146)	(7,995)	(44,857)	(31,983)	(18,668)	4,527	10,084	35,291	(199,999)
EXTRAORDINARY INCOME/ (EXPENSE)	0	0	0	0	0	0	0	0	0	0	0	0	0

(continues)

Exhibit 11.5 *continued*

	Jan.	Feb.	Mar.	Apr.	May	June	July	Aug.	Sept.	Oct.	Nov.	Dec.	12 Months
EARNINGS BEFORE INTEREST AND TAXES	(35,005)	(26,511)	(20,373)	(37,363)	(27,146)	(7,995)	(44,857)	(31,983)	(18,668)	4,527	10,084	35,291	(199,999)
INTEREST INCOME/(EXPENSE)	0	0	0	0	0	0	0	0	0	0	0	0	0
NET EARNINGS BEFORE TAXES	(35,005)	(26,511)	(20,373)	(37,363)	(27,146)	(7,995)	(44,857)	(31,983)	(18,668)	4,527	10,084	35,291	(199,999)
TAXES	0	0	0	0	0	0	0	0	0	0	0	0	0
NET EARNINGS	(35,005)	(26,511)	(20,373)	(37,363)	(27,146)	(7,995)	(44,857)	(31,983)	(18,668)	4,527	10,084	35,291	(199,999)

FireFly Toys Income Statement Year 2 by Months

	Jan.	Feb.	Mar.	Apr.	May	June	July	Aug.	Sept.	Oct.	Nov.	Dec.	Total 12 Months
REVENUES	137,380	220,530	245,840	300,070	368,760	368,760	354,300	433,840	404,920	484,460	524,230	524,230	4,367,320
COST OF REVENUE	40,748	65,411	72,918	89,003	109,376	109,376	105,087	128,680	120,102	143,694	155,490	155,490	1,295,373
GROSS PROFIT	96,632	155,119	172,922	211,067	259,384	259,384	249,213	305,160	284,818	340,766	368,740	368,740	3,071,947

OPERATING EXPENSES

Sales and marketing	113,345	109,345	109,345	109,345	109,345	109,345	109,345	109,345	109,345	109,345	109,345	109,345	1,316,138
Research and development	6,083	6,083	6,083	6,083	6,083	6,083	6,083	6,083	6,083	6,083	6,083	6,083	73,000
General and administration	44,133	44,133	44,133	44,133	44,133	44,133	44,133	44,133	44,133	44,133	44,133	44,133	529,599
Total operating expenses	163,561	159,561	159,561	159,561	159,561	159,561	159,561	159,561	159,561	159,561	159,561	159,561	1,918,737
EARNINGS FROM OPERATIONS	(66,929)	(4,442)	13,361	51,506	99,822	99,822	89,651	145,599	125,257	181,205	209,179	209,179	1,153,210
EXTRAORDINARY INCOME/(EXPENSE)	0	0	0	0	0	0	0	0	0	0	0	0	0
EARNINGS BEFORE INTEREST AND TAXES	(66,929)	(4,442)	13,361	51,506	99,822	99,822	89,651	145,599	125,257	181,205	209,179	209,179	1,153,210
INTEREST INCOME/(EXPENSE)	(1,500)	(1,500)	(1,500)	(1,500)	(1,500)	(1,500)	(1,500)	(1,500)	(1,500)	(1,500)	(1,500)	(1,500)	(18,000)
NET EARNINGS BEFORE TAXES	(68,429)	(5,942)	11,861	50,006	98,322	98,322	88,151	144,099	123,757	179,705	207,679	207,679	1,135,210
TAXES	22,549	1,958	(3,909)	(16,478)	(32,400)	(32,400)	(29,048)	(47,485)	(40,781)	(59,218)	(68,436)	(68,436)	(374,084)
NET EARNINGS	(45,880)	(3,984)	7,952	33,528	65,922	65,922	59,103	96,614	82,975	120,487	139,243	139,243	761,126

11.2 The Cash Flow Statement

FireFly is raising $695,000 in equity financing in year 1 on top of the $55,000 already raised. Series A will close in January 2003 for $320,000. Series B will close in August 2003 for $375,000. In year 2 the Company will seek a line of credit to finance inventories and working capital. Exhibit 11.6 shows the cash flow statement for 5 years, and Exhibit 11.7 shows cash flow monthly for the first two years.

> "Cash is king." It is a good idea to lay out the funding timing. Cash flow needs to be monthly because it is critical to see when cash gets low.

11.3 The Balance Sheet

Exhibit 11.8 provides the overall pro forma annual balance sheet for years 1 through 5. Accounts receivables will be outstanding an average of 30 days. Plant, property, and equipment consist of computers and office furnishings. All manufacturing will be outsourced. Liabilities will consist of accounts payable and short-term credit lines to finance inventories. The company will use equity for the majority of its start-up costs. To establish a new niche in children's toys and grow the opportunity, FireFly will not pay out a dividend for the foreseeable future. To date FireFly has raised $55,000 from friends and family.

Exhibit 11.6 *Cash Flow Statement Years 1 to 5*

	2003	2004	2005	2006	2007
OPERATING ACTIVITIES					
Net earnings	(200,000)	771,926	1,789,528	3,237,867	4,557,238
Depreciation	3,667	13,667	25,000	46,667	70,000
Working capital changes					
(Increase)/decrease accounts receivable	(215,972)	(308,258)	(473,597)	(638,697)	(755,615)
(Increase)/decrease inventories	(180,655)	(611,000)	(400,663)	(600,994)	(901,491)
(Increase)/decrease other current assets	0	0	0	0	0
Increase/(decrease) accts pay and accrd expenses	215,108	307,025	471,702	636,142	752,593
Increase/(decrease) other current liab	0	0	0	0	0
Net cash provided/(used) by operating activities	(377,852)	173,360	1,411,971	2,680,985	3,722,725
INVESTING ACTIVITIES					
Property and equipment	(11,000)	(30,000)	(45,000)	(65,000)	(100,000)
Net cash used in investing activities	(11,000)	(30,000)	(45,000)	(65,000)	(100,000)
FINANCING ACTIVITIES					
Increase/(decrease) short-term debt	0	0	0	0	0
Increase/(decrease) curr. portion LTD	0	0	0	0	0
Increase/(decrease) long-term debt	0	0	0	0	0
Increase/(decrease) common stock	0	0	0	0	0
Increase/(decrease) preferred stock	695,000	0	0	0	0
Dividends declared	0	0	0	0	0
Net cash provided/(used) by financing	695,000	0	0	0	0
INCREASE/(DECREASE) IN CASH	306,148	143,360	1,366,971	2,615,985	3,622,725
CASH AT BEGINNING OF YEAR	6,000	312,148	455,508	1,822,479	4,438,464
CASH AT END OF YEAR	312,148	455,508	1,822,479	4,438,464	8,061,189

Cash is very high, but this probably is attributable to the low operating expense forecasts, which we think are too optimistic.

Exhibit 11.7 Cash Flow Statement Year 1 by Months ($)

	Jan.	Feb.	Mar.	Apr.	May	June	July	Aug.	Sept.	Oct.	Nov.	Dec.	Year 1
OPERATING ACTIVITIES													
Net earnings	(35,005)	(26,511)	(20,373)	(37,363)	(27,146)	(7,995)	(44,857)	(31,983)	(18,668)	4,527	10,084	35,291	(199,999)
Depreciation	306	306	306	306	306	306	306	306	306	306	306	306	3,667
Working capital changes													
(Increase)/ decrease AR	(520)	(1,040)	(260)	(3,119)	(5,195)	(31,458)	(6,24 0)	(19,765)	(20,780)	(57,175)	(15,600)	(54,822)	(215,972)
(Increase)/ decrease inventories	0	614	754	1,981	(66,719)	(17,650)	12,100	(26,500)	(10,750)	(116,750)	(16,735)	59,000	(180,655)
(Increase)/ decrease other current assets	0	0	0	0	0	0	0	0	0	0	0	0	0
(Increase)/ decrease in prepaids	0	0	0	0	0	0	0	0	0	0	0	0	0
Accts pay and accrd expenses	517	1,036	259	3,106	5,174	31,332	6,215	19,686	20,697	56,946	15,538	54,603	215,108
Increase/ (decrease) other current liab	0	0	0	0	0	0	0	0	0	0	0	0	0

Net cash provided/ (used) by operating activities	(34,702)	(25,596)	(19,315)	(35,088)	(93,580)	(25,465)	(32,477)	(58,256)	(29,195)	(112,146)	(6,408)	94,378	(377,851)
INVESTING ACTIVITIES													
Property and equipment	(917)	(917)	(917)	(917)	(917)	(917)	(917)	(917)	(917)	(917)	(917)	(917)	(11,000)
Other													0
Net cash used in investing activities	(917)	(917)	(917)	(917)	(917)	(917)	(917)	(917)	(917)	(917)	(917)	(917)	(11,000)
FINANCING ACTIVITIES													
Short-term debt	0												0
Curr. portion LTD	0												0
Long-term debt	0												0
Common stock	0												0
Preferred stock	320,000							375,000					695,000
Dividends declared													0
Net cash provided/(used)	320,000	0	0	0	0	0	0	375,000	0	375,000	0	0	695,000
INCREASE/ (DECREASE) IN CASH	284,382	(26,513)	(20,231)	(36,005)	(94,497)	(26,382)	(33,393)	315,827	(30,112)	(113,063)	(7,325)	93,461	306,149

(continues)

137

Exhibit 11.7 continued

	Jan.	Feb.	Mar.	Apr.	May	June	July	Aug.	Sept.	Oct.	Nov.	Dec.	Year 1
CASH AT BEGINNING OF PERIOD	6,000	290,382	263,869	243,637	207,633	113,136	86,754	53,361	369,188	339,076	226,013	218,688	
CASH AT END OF PERIOD	290,382	263,869	243,637	207,633	113,136	86,754	53,361	369,188	339,076	226,013	218,688	312,149	

Note that without the second round of financing, FireFly would run out of cash at this point in time.

Cash Flow Statement Year 2 by Months ($)

	Jan.	Feb.	Mar.	Apr.	May	June	July	Aug.	Sept.	Oct.	Nov.	Dec.	Estimated Year 2
OPERATING ACTIVITIES													
Net earnings	(44,800)	(2,973)	8,943	34,477	66,818	66,818	60,010	97,460	83,843	121,293	140,018	140,018	771,926
Depreciation	1,139	1,139	1,139	1,139	1,139	1,139	1,139	1,139	1,139	1,139	1,139	1,139	13,667
Working capital changes (Increase)/decrease accounts receivable	78,592	(83,150)	(25,310)	(54,230)	(68,690)	0	14,460	(79,540)	28,920	(79,540)	(39,770)	0	(308,258)

	C1	C2	C3	C4	C5	C6	C7	C8	C9	C10	C11	C12	C13
(Increase)/decrease inventories	61,750	(266,750)	88,750	109,000	(37,375)	(291,875)	154,250	7,000	179,250	(996,750)	203,375	178,375	(611,000)
(Increase)/decrease other current assets	0	0	0	0	0	0	0	0	0	0	0	0	0
Prepaid expenses							0		0	0			
Accts pay and accrd expenses	(78,278)	82,817	25,209	54,013	68,415	0	(14,402)	79,222	(28,804)	79,222	39,611	0	307,025
Increase/(decrease) other current liab	0	0	0	0	0	0	0	0	0	0	0	0	0
Net cash provided/(used) by operating activities	18,403	(268,917)	98,731	144,399	30,307	(223,918)	215,457	105,281	264,348	(874,636)	344,373	319,532	173,360

INVESTING ACTIVITIES

	C1	C2	C3	C4	C5	C6	C7	C8	C9	C10	C11	C12	C13
Property and equipment	(2,500)	(2,500)	(2,500)	(2,500)	(2,500)	(2,500)	(2,500)	(2,500)	(2,500)	(2,500)	(2,500)	(2,500)	(30,000)
Other													0
Net cash used in investing activities	(2,500)	(2,500)	(2,500)	(2,500)	(2,500)	(2,500)	(2,500)	(2,500)	(2,500)	(2,500)	(2,500)	(2,500)	(30,000)

(continues)

Exhibit 11.7 continued

	Jan.	Feb.	Mar.	Apr.	May	June	July	Aug.	Sept.	Oct.	Nov.	Dec.	Year 1
FINANCING ACTIVITIES													
Increase/(decrease) short-term debt													0
Increase/(decrease) curr. Portion LTD	0											0	0
Increase/(decrease) long-term debt	0											0	0
Increase/(decrease) common stock	0									250,000	(250,000)	0	0
Increase/(decrease) preferred stock	0											0	0
Dividends declared	0											0	0
Net cash provided/(used)	0	0	0	0	0	0	0	0	0	250,000	(250,000)	0	0
INCREASE/(DECREASE) IN CASH	15,903	(271,417)	96,231	141,899	27,807	(226,418)	212,957	102,781	261,848	(627,136)	91,873	317,032	143,360
CASH AT BEGINNING OF PERIOD	312,149	328,052	56,635	152,866	294,765	322,572	96,154	309,111	411,891	673,739	46,603	138,477	
CASH AT END OF PERIOD	328,052	56,635	152,866	294,765	322,572	96,154	309,111	411,891	673,739	46,603	138,477	455,509	

A line of credit prevents FireFly from running out of cash here. It is common for companies to finance their production cycle, but it is harder to do that without an operating history. This is likely why FireFly uses equity in year 1 and then seeks debt in year 2.

Exhibit 11.8 Balance Sheet Years 1 to 5 ($)

	Begin	2003	2004	2005	2006	2007
ASSETS						
CURRENT ASSETS						
Cash	6,000	312,148	455,508	1,822,479	4,438,464	8,061,189
Accounts receivable	0	215,972	524,230	997,827	1,636,523	2,392,138
Inventories	9,670	190,325	801,325	1,201,988	1,802,981	2,704,472
Other current assets	0	0	0	0	0	0
						0
Total current assets	15,670	718,445	1,781,063	4,022,293	7,877,968	13,157,799
PROPERTY AND EQUIPMENT	0	7,333	23,667	43,667	62,000	92,000
TOTAL ASSETS	15,670	725,779	1,804,729	4,065,960	7,939,968	13,249,799
LIABILITIES AND SHAREHOLDERS' EQUITY						
CURRENT LIABILITIES						
Short-term debt	0	0	0	0	0	0
Accounts payable and accrued expenses	0	235,108	542,133	1,013,835	1,649,977	2,402,570

(continues)

141

Exhibit 11.8 *continued*

	Begin	2003	2004	2005	2006	2007
Other current liab	0	0	0	0	0	0
Current portion of long-term debt		0	0	0	0	0
Total current liabilities	0	235,108	542,133	1,013,835	1,649,977	2,402,570
LONG-TERM DEBT (less current portion)	0	0	0	0	0	0
STOCKHOLDERS' EQUITY						
Common stock	55,000	55,000	55,000	55,000	55,000	55,000
Preferred stock	0	695,000	695,000	695,000	695,000	695,000
Retained earnings	(39,330)	(259,330)	512,596	2,302,125	5,539,991	10,097,229
	15,670	490,670	1,262,596	3,052,125	6,289,991	10,847,229
TOTAL LIABILITIES AND EQUITY	15,670	725,779	1,804,729	4,065,960	7,939,968	13,249,799

Appendices: Adding Bells and Whistles

The appendices can include anything that you think adds validation to your concept but doesn't fit or is too large to insert in the main parts of the plan. Common inclusions would be one-page résumés of key team members, articles that feature your venture, technical specifications, and the like. FireFly included reprints of the *Time* magazine and *Boston Business Journal* articles that highlighted the company.[2] FireFly also includes its brochure and other marketing materials. Due to space constraints, these appendices aren't included in this book.

Chapter Summary

Financial projections are an art. You can never predict the future precisely, but you need to anticipate what can happen. Financial projections help you gauge the attractiveness of the opportunity. What is the profit potential? How might the company grow? What does this mean for you, your team, your employees, and your investors? In summary, financial projections are the numbers equivalent of the story you have articulated in the rest of the plan. Just like the written plan, the financial statements need revisiting and refining as you learn more about the opportunity. We believe it is imperative for you, the lead entrepreneur, to own the numbers. If you rely on others, you won't be able to make strong decisions about how to proceed or raise the money you need to get started. Although building and understanding financial statements can require effort for those of you who are less proficient in numbers, the time you take to familiarize yourself with the financials is time well spent.

---

[2]If you are interested in seeing the articles, go to http://www.time.com/time/ and http://www.bizjournals.com/boston/. We did not have room to reprint them in this book.

11 CONCLUSION

FireFly Epilogue

The FireFly plan we have used throughout this book is an actual plan produced by an entrepreneur trying to launch her business. It is the third major iteration of the plan, quite different from the initial draft completed in December 2001 and probably very different from the next iteration. During each major draft the entrepreneur's sophistication in describing the concept and the opportunity improves. It is useful to map how the business has evolved over time. Below are the major changes (items 1 through 6 are included in the business plan in this book; items 7 and 8 have evolved since that time):

1. Wants to start a business that helps children.
2. Develops a plush toy concept geared toward unaccompanied children flying on planes.
3. Expands concept to include children in distress (facing divorce of parents or illness or death of close family member).
4. Adds story book about the Comfort Creature facing a stressful situation.
5. Adds Comfort Kits to go along with Comfort Creatures.
6. Recognizes that penetrating the specialty toy store channel is difficult and devises alternative distribution strategy (hospitals and other organizations that work with children).
7. Through selling product, finds that buyers aren't clear on how to use product, and so develops a caregiver's guide.

8. Develops training program to deliver to professional caregivers. The program may generate some revenue, but the main benefit is that it drives product sales.

Each iteration suggests that Lauren has gained a much deeper understanding of how to reach her core customer: children in distress. During her investigation of the toy industry Lauren came to appreciate the difficulty of penetrating the mainstream distribution channels. She also learned that the failure rate of new toy products is high. But working with children is Lauren's passion, and she was not easily dissuaded. Lauren needed a strategy that might help overcome the long odds; she needed to go through the business planning process. Lauren learned that a key to successful business planning process is talking—talking to anybody and everybody you can. These conversations build your knowledge and network and put you in a better position to take *action*.

Lauren has been a master networker. She offers this advice: "Be willing to talk to everybody. When you speak with someone, ask for names of other people to talk to. Everybody, even those who don't seem like relevant contacts, has insight that can help. Once you have spoken with someone, follow up with e-mails thanking that person and then e-mail the people he or she told you to contact, copying the original person." Lauren has found that almost everybody is reachable through e-mail, and she has been surprised at how cold contacts will respond through e-mail. Lauren relates the following story on how networking has led to strong leads:

> One of my contacts suggested I call this woman in New York. I didn't have any idea how this woman might be relevant to my venture, but I secured a 30-minute meeting anyway. The woman introduced me to another woman who worked for a PR firm that handled the Toy Industry Association. That woman put me in contact with CEOs from very large toy companies. It is too early to see where this may lead, but building my network in this industry can only help.

As this excerpt illustrates, entrepreneurs who talk and network not only improve their vision but also find potential partners and advisers. Who should you talk to? The list starts with the smartest people in the industry. Who are the world-class experts you will emulate or hope to surpass? It includes potential customers, distributors, vendors, advisers, mentors, and even competitors. Very early in the process you should define who your core customer is in terms of demographics (age, gender, income, etc.) and psychographics (what motivates the person to buy). During such interactions Lauren learned to appreciate who buys Comfort Creatures and Comfort Kits for children (users of the product). She learned that the obvious buyer, the parent, may not be the only or best target customer. By talking to preschool teachers, child psychologists, counselors, and others who interact with children, Lauren learned that they were looking for more tools to help a child communicate. Through her contacts Lauren was able to set up focus groups with children. During those sessions Lauren observed how children interact with toys and with caregivers. Those sessions, along with consultations with caregivers, led to one of the Comfort Creature's distinctive attributes: the feeling pouch. Lauren also learned that there may be a better way to reach these caregivers than the traditional retail distribution channels: direct sales to the organizations where the caregivers work. Those conversations also fostered advisers. FireFly's board of advisers is filled with customers who have become evangelists who help spread the word of FireFly's benefits.

Lauren has spent considerable time talking to people who work in her distribution channels. Early in the process Lauren visited several specialty toy retailers and learned how they acquire products to sell. Through those interactions she secured some test sites (stores that were willing to display her toys). This information will provide Lauren with valuable knowledge on a number of fronts. First, should FireFly even use this channel? It has become a secondary channel in the early stages of the company, but Lauren believes specialty toy stores may be a mechanism for rapid growth once the product builds recognition through other channels. Thus, she is testing the channel in anticipation of future growth. Through this test Lauren hopes to learn how FireFly should position its product in the store. Second, how does the end customer perceive the product? Third, are specialty retail stores an appropriate channel, or should FireFly focus solely on the institutional channel? Lauren can spend time in the store and observe which customers look at the FireFly products, which customers buy the products, and so forth. Based on that intelligence, FireFly can adapt and reposition the product if necessary. Lauren also has spent time talking to philanthropic organizations, hospitals, and schools. Through these conversations, she has learned that she needs to support caregivers in determining how best to use the product. To that end she is designing "train the caregiver" seminars. She also has learned that many organizations have budgets for such training. Thus, this may develop into another revenue stream for the company.

Vendors are also fruitful providers of information. Vendors helped Lauren understand the production process and ways to make the highest-quality product at a reasonable price. But vendors' knowledge goes beyond that. Through conversations with vendors, you can learn about best practices. These vendors may supply your competitors. Although vendors never divulge trade secrets—nor should you press them to—you can gain insight into how your competitors operate. If you are doing an innovative product—one that you believe nobody else has ever done—you may learn through vendors of stealth competitors, companies in the prelaunch period that have yet to sell a product or service. Vendors often are knowledgeable about other suppliers you might need and what distribution channels might work and can provide a different perspective on what your customer wants. It is never too early to start talking to potential vendors.

By talking to everybody and anybody, you can build up a list of advisers and mentors who can help you with a wide array of business issues. Lauren has done an excellent job of broadening her advisers beyond child-care professionals. She has leveraged all her business school professors (including us) by meeting with them outside class and even after her graduation. She used her network to identify a lawyer who helped her in contracting with vendors and investors and also provided advice on intellectual property protection (copyright, trademark, etc.) for lower fees than she would have paid if she had arranged it through the phone book. More recently she has encouraged a leading family business accountant to join her board of advisers (and even invest). Entrepreneurs who talk are more likely to move the business forward than are paranoid entrepreneurs who believe everybody is out to steal their idea.

It is even possible to talk to your competitors by attending trade shows. As soon as Lauren conceived her idea, she started attending toy trade shows. Through those events she met many entrepreneurs who were similar to her. They had innovative toy products and had launched them. Those entrepreneurs gave her invaluable advice on the hurdles she would face and how she might overcome them. Lauren also identified potential partners. For instance, Comfort Kits incorporate other toys into the package. Many of these contacts remain informal advisers to FireFly. In addition to toy trade shows, Lauren attends conventions that attract professional child caregivers. The key is to view the business planning process as one of gathering information that will help you move the business forward and succeed.

As we are writing this book (May 2004), FireFly continues to make progress toward entering the market. The company is close to securing its next round of financing. One investor has agreed to put up $70,000 of the $320,000 FireFly is seeking provided that Lauren can secure the other investors. This type of pledge is called a soft commitment and is very common when one is seeking funds. Closing this round of financing won't ensure FireFly's success. In fact, we may not know for many years if FireFly will be a sustainable business, but the process Lauren has gone through has increased her chances. She is passionate and articulate about her opportunity. Without going through the business planning process, Lauren wouldn't be clear about her business model and wouldn't have been able to persuade the investors to date ($110,000) or the ones she is seeking now to believe in her vision. Business planning will help you gain that deep understanding necessary to articulate your vision convincingly and get buy-in from investors, customers, team members, and so forth.

Next Steps If You Need Funding

Once you have a strong draft of your business plan, you are in a better position to seek outside funding. However, most investors, whether they are venture capitalists, angels, friends, or family members, do not want to see your completed plan, at least not initially. What they want is often a dehydrated plan (5 to 10 pages) and 5 to 10 PowerPoint slides. Many investors will ask you to e-mail them the summary and slides in advance of their possibly asking you in for a meeting. They want something short and concise to get a sense of the opportunity (Is it attractive? Is it something they normally invest in?), a good sense of the team (Are you capable of executing the opportunity?), and how the investment will help you move the business to the next level. If the investors are excited after reading your summary and reviewing your slides, they probably will ask you in to discuss the opportunity. Think of the stand-alone summary and PowerPoint slides as a hook. You are trying to entice the investors to learn more. If the meeting goes well and the investor is still interested, she may ask for the full plan. Many investors use the business plan as a road map to conduct due diligence—to investigate whether your claims are valid or just a pipe dream. But before you can get there, you need to hook the investor.

The dehydrated business plan is derived from the full business plan.[1] First and foremost, you need to add a cover page similar to the one you have included with the business plan. Add visuals such as product pictures, competitor maps, and customer profiles. In addition to filling out details in all the subsections of the plan, provide as much information on the team as possible. Harkening back to the old adage that investors prefer to back A-level teams with B ideas versus B teams with A ideas, you need to convince them that you can execute the opportunity. In Appendix 3 we evaluate the Fossa dehydrated business plan. In other words, Gloria Ro Kolb, the Fossa founder, could send that executive summary (dehydrated plan) to an investor without the business plan, and the investor would be able to understand the business and make a preliminary assessment of whether it was worth further investigation.

Creating PowerPoint slides is a valuable exercise because it forces you to think about your opportunity visually. The 12 or so slides should cover the following areas:

1. Cover page showing product picture, company name, and contact information
2. Opportunity description emphasizing customer problem or need you hope to solve
3. Your product or service, illustrating how it solves the customer's problem
4. Some details (as needed) to describe your product better
5. Competition overview
6. Your entry and growth strategy, showing how you will get into the industry and then grow
7. Overview of your business model, meaning how you make money and how much it costs to support those sales
8. Team description

---

[1]Remember that in Chapter 1 we suggested that the first step you might take is to write a dehydrated plan because it is a good document to share with team members and other trusted advisers who can help you develop your business. The dehydrated plan you write at the end of the business planning process is much more articulate than the previous version. It has the ability to hook investors.

9. Current status with timeline
10. Summary, including how much you need and how that money will be used

A mistake entrepreneurs often make in creating PowerPoint slides is using too much text. Bullet point slides are easy to create but aren't as compelling as pictures. A picture is truly worth a thousand words, and so your challenge is to substitute visuals for words whenever possible. Appendix 4 shows PowerPoint slides for Fossa Medical. It should be noted that these slides are "build" slides,[2] meaning that although there are only 14 of them, a few have parts that animate in based on what Gloria is talking about.

Fossa Medical Prologue

Fossa Medical was started by Babson College MBA Gloria Ro Kolb. The business plan we are illustrating is one that Gloria wrote as she was seeking a round of financing for $3.7 million. As you will read in the business plan, Fossa Medical has a patented device that will change how people are treated for kidney stones. The company already has raised $425,000. The initial funding was used for animal trials and U.S. Food and Drug Administration (FDA) clearance. The company has been completing human trials and launched the product in 2003.

As you read through the Fossa plan, you will notice that it is different from FireFly's plan on several fronts. The most obvious difference is that the plan is about a technology business. Fossa is a year older than FireFly, and Gloria has gone through a half dozen iterations of the planning process. In certain respects the plan is more concise and developed. The plan also varies somewhat from the format we lead you through in this book. Gloria presents the company first, for example. Remember, the business planning process is for your benefit, and if you want to modify the order of the material, the depth of the discussion, or other aspects, that is fine as long as you get the learning you need. We can't stress enough how important it is to view the business planning process as an ongoing learning cycle. You should go through several iterations and refine the plan based on its purpose. You don't necessarily need to

---

[2] "Build" slides bring in additional elements at the click of a mouse.

re-create a new written document each time, but you should refine your thinking on and execution of different aspects of the business continually. As you read through the Fossa plan, think about the process that Gloria was going through. Think about the questions she uncovered and evaluate how well the plan has answered those questions. Compare that with the stage of development for the FireFly plan. What differences do you see? Just as with FireFly, we will annotate aspects of the plan that we think do a good job and others that might be improved.

Just as was the case with FireFly, it is too early to tell if Fossa will be a sustainable business. Yet the additional milestones that Fossa has passed (due to its longer existence) make it that much closer to becoming an ongoing entity. Fossa has built a strong team and seems well positioned to enter the market. Launching a business isn't a sprint; it's a marathon. We expect that your business planning process will help you train to run that race.

Beyond the Business Plan

There is much debate about the value of a business plan. We even proclaim that the plan will be obsolete as soon as it comes off the press! Some have suggested that 5 or 10 PowerPoint slides, a "dehydrated" plan, or an executive summary is all that is needed. These are important extracts from the business plan, but the argument about whether you need a business plan is a red herring. Most of the debate is really about communicating the contents of the plan, not about business planning. This book helps you travel along a very personal entrepreneurial journey in a manner that will focus your energies. The true value of crafting a business plan is that it imposes the discipline that allows you to become an expert on your industry and your idea for making that industry better. Ultimately, the business planning process helps you shape your ideas into concrete, executable opportunities that create value. This process—the hard work of new venture due diligence and articulation—is a learnable skill that makes you a better entrepreneur. Remember, the deep understanding of your opportunity is the competitive advantage you will need to push the odds of success in your favor. At the same time it will help you raise money, recruit key management, secure vendors, and attract customers.

Although this book lays out the business plan as a sequential process, you must remember that it is iterative. Writing one section has implications for the other sections, and you will find yourself revisiting those sections continuously. That is why it doesn't matter that the business plan is obsolete the minute it comes out of the printer. Harkening back to Chapter 1, where we talked about the Timmons Model, the planning process helps you do the following:

1. Gauge the nature of the opportunity
2. Shape that opportunity and create a plan to launch and grow the business
3. Enhance your ability to articulate the value-creating potential of your company

Having worked with hundreds of entrepreneurs throughout the years, we are always impressed by the tangible growth in the clarity of the entrepreneur's vision during the business planning process. The process forces you to ask and answer important questions. It helps you identify the critical assumptions, or leaps of faith, that must occur for the business to succeed. Once you understand those assumptions, you can take steps to reduce the uncertainty around them. More knowledge will enhance your chances of success.

Conclusion

Welcome to the entrepreneurial revolution. We hope you have found this book useful as you embark on your entrepreneurial endeavor. By going through the business planning process, you will improve your chances of success. The process and discipline put you in charge of evaluating and shaping choices and initiating action that makes sense rather than just letting things happen. Having a longer-term sense of direction is highly motivating. It is also extremely helpful in determining when to say no (which is much harder than saying yes) and can replace impulsive hunches with a more thoughtful strategic purpose.

When you have launched your business, you will contribute to the country's economic vitality. We hope your business will create jobs not just for you but for others. Your business may well be a lasting legacy that outlives you. Remember to think big. Companies that grow will survive and prosper. Because of their innovative nature and competitive breakthroughs, entrepreneurial ventures have demonstrated a remarkable capacity to invent new paradigms of organization and management. They have abandoned the organizational practices and structures typical of the industrial giants from the post–World War II era to the 1990s. The world needs big problems solved and has relied on entrepreneurs to find those solutions. Think of Henry Ford, Thomas Watson (IBM), Bill Gates, and Home Depot's Arthur Blank. Your business may never reach the size of those firms (nor may you have such aspirations), but you will have a lasting impact on your family and community. Enjoy the trip.

Appendices

1 Quick Screen Exercise

I. Market- and Margin-Related Issues

Criterion	Higher Potential	Lower Potential
Need/want/problem	Identified	Unfocused
Customers	Reachable & receptive	Unreachable/loyal to others
Payback to users	<1 year	>3 years
Value added or created	IRR 40% +	IRR < 20%
Market size	$50–$100 million	<$10 million or +1 billion
Market growth rate	+20%	Less than 20%, contracting
Gross margin	40%+ and durable	Less than 20% and fragile
Overall potential:		
1. Market	higher _____	avg _____ lower
2. Margins	higher _____	avg _____ lower

II. Competitive Advantages

	Higher Potential	Lower Potential
Fixed and variable costs	Highest >>>>>>>>>>>>>>>>>>> Lowest	
Degree of control	Stronger >>>>>>>>>>>>>>>> Weaker	
Prices and cost		
Channels of supply and		
distribution		
Barriers to entry	Strong >>>>>>>>>>>>>>>>>>> None	
Proprietary advantage		
Lead time advantage (product,		
technology, people, resources,		
location)		
Service chain		
Contractual advantage		
Contacts and networks		
Overall Potential		

1. Costs	higher _____avg_____ lower
2. Channel	higher _____avg_____ lower
3. Barriers to entry	higher _____avg_____ lower
4. Timing	higher _____avg_____ lower

III. Value Creation and Realization Issues

	Higher Potential	Lower Potential
Profit after tax	10–15% or more and durable	<5%; fragile
Time to breakeven	<2 years	>3 years
Time to positive cash flow	<2 years	>3 years
ROI potential	40–70% +, durable	<20%, fragile
Value	High strategic value	Low strategic value
Capitalization requirements	Low-moderate; fundable	Very high; difficult to fund
Exit mechanism	IPO, acquisition	Undefined; illiquid investment

Overall value creation potential
  1. Timing   higher _____avg_____ lower
  2. Profit/free   higher _____avg_____ lower
     cash flow
  3. Exit/liquidity   higher _____avg_____ lower

IV. Overall Potential

	Go	No Go	Go, if . . .
1. Margins and markets			
2. Competitive advantages			
3. Value creation and realization			
4. Fit: "O" + "R" + "T"			
5. Risk-reward balance			
6. Timing			
7. Other compelling issues: must know or likely to fail			

  a.
  b.
  c.
  d.
  e.

2 Business Plan Guide Exercise

Name:

Venture:

Data:

STEP 1 Segment Information into Key Sections

Establish priorities for each section, including individual responsibilities and due dates for drafts and the final version. When you segment your information, it is vital to keep in mind that the plan needs to be logically integrated and that information should be consistent. Note that since the market opportunity section is the heart and soul of the plan, it may be the most difficult section to write; however, it is best to assign it a high priority and begin working there first. Remember to include tasks such as printing in the list.

Section or Task	Priority	Person(s) Responsible	Date to Begin	First Draft Due Date	Date Completed or Final Version Due Date

STEP 2 List Tasks That Need to Be Completed

Devise an overall schedule for preparing the plan by assigning priority, persons responsible, and due dates to each task necessary to complete the plan. It is helpful to break larger items (field work to gather customer and competitor intelligence, trade show visits, etc.) into small, more manageable components (such as phone calls required before a trip can be taken) and to include the components as tasks. *Be as specific as possible.*

Task	Priority	Person(s) Responsible	Date to Begin	Date of Completion

STEP 3 Combine the List of Segments and the List of Tasks to Create a Calendar

In combining your lists, consider if anything has been omitted and whether you have been realistic in what people can do, when they can do it, what needs to be done, and so forth. To create your calendar, place an X in the week when the task is to be started and an X in the week when it is to be completed and then connect the X's. When you have placed all tasks on the calendar, look carefully for conflicts or lack of realism. In particular, evaluate if team members are overscheduled.

Task	Week														
	1	2	3	4	5	6	7	8	9	10	11	12	13	14	15

STEP 4 A Framework to Develop and Write a Business Plan

While preparing your plan you most likely will want to consider sections in an order different from the one presented in this book. Also, when you integrate your sections into the final plan, you may choose to present material somewhat differently. The key is to make it *your* plan.

3 Fossa Business Plan

Gloria Ro Kolb, Founder and President
Fossa Medical, Inc.
580 Harrison Ave.
4th Floor
Boston, MA 02118
617-275-7480
www.fossamedical.com

Dated: July 17, 2002

The components of this business plan have been submitted on a confidential basis. It may not be reproduced, stored, or copied in any form. By accepting delivery of this plan, the recipient agrees to return this copy of the plan. Do not copy, fax, reproduce, or distribute without permission.

Copy 2 of 5

Good use of major section headings and subheadings. Note that the implementation plan (page 21) combines elements of the marketing, operations, and development plans. Fossa varies from the discussed format primarily due to the stage of its development. It is still in product development and approval (this can be a lengthy process for medical devices), and so it doesn't have as well developed a marketing plan as would a business that has a product that is ready to launch. Also note that intellectual property, regulatory, and reimbursement issues are critical risks faced by Fossa.

TABLE OF CONTENTS

EXECUTIVE SUMMARY

Overview

Fossa Medical (the "Company" or "Fossa") develops and markets innovative products focused on conditions that affect the small passageways of the body. Our patented technology keeps passageways open and removes obstructions like kidney stones and gallstones. Fossa's technologies offer substantial benefits over those of existing devices, including improved patient outcomes and lower cost of care.

Initially Fossa will target the removal of kidney stones, as this clinical application provides a significant market opportunity. Longer term, our technology is applicable to the following areas:

* Removal of stones in the common bile duct
* Restoring normal function to urinary and biliary tracts compressed by a tumor.

Market Opportunity

* 10% of Americans suffer excruciating pain from kidney stones at some point in their lives, nearly 2 million cases each year.
* $2 billion is spent annually removing kidney stones
* 250,000 procedures each year treat primarily medium-size and large stones—no treatment is currently offered for small stones because it is hoped that they eventually will pass naturally.
* Current treatments are slow and ineffective, often necessitating multiple interventions, which increase the cost and invasiveness of patient management.

> The bullets highlight Fossa's "hook." There is a customer need and a large market, and Fossa can do it better. We would like to see where these figures (i.e., $2 billion) came from. It is a good idea to footnote sources of data.

Fossa's technology works in conjunction with existing technologies to remove large stones and offers a procedure to remove small stones that are currently untreated, thereby reducing the pain suffered by these patients.

Fossa's first product, the Fossa Stone Sweeper™, will be marketed as a complement to extracorporeal shock wave lithotripsy (ESWL) procedures and as a replacement for most ureteroscopy procedures. Medical Data International confirms that devices such as the Sweeper™, which are used to make ESWL treatment more effective, are likely to be the largest area of growth in the stone market. The Company projects that this device market is $180 million in the United States and over $500 million worldwide.

Fossa will adapt the product for use in two other medical markets: removal of stones in the common bile duct (75,000 procedures performed annually in the US) and management of tumors that compress the ureter (60,000 procedures annually). Altogether, Fossa projects a $750M worldwide market for its initial products.

Sizes the market in concrete terms that allow investors to judge the attractiveness of the venture; however, we again would like to know the source for these figures.

Introduces growth strategy. Enter two additional markets.

Products

Lays out product features. Bullets visually draw attention and highlight key benefits of product.

Fossa Medical has developed a unique product that can reduce the time, pain, and uncertainty of stone removal. The product, called the Stone Sweeper™, can

- Passively dilate the ureter, trapping and removing stones in a fashion similar to the currently used basket retrievers, thus minimizing the need to retrain physicians for its use.
- Be used with ESWL to speed stone removal after stones are fragmented.
- Replace current first-line therapies such as stents and baskets.
- Remove 3- to 5-mm stones that currently do not get treatment but still pass too slowly.
- Be used in pregnant women.

Ultimately, the greatest advantage of Fossa's product is the resulting dilated passageway that will enable the quick removal of stones outside of the operating room, thus saving time, procedure costs, and inpatient stay.

Sweeper™ in Insertion and Expanded Forms

Picture of product draws attention and implies the stage of development.

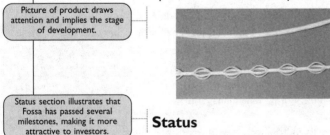

Status

Status section illustrates that Fossa has passed several milestones, making it more attractive to investors.

- FDA market clearance of the first indication was granted on June 28, 2002.
- Design is frozen; engineering is complete.
- Prototypes of the Fossa Sweeper™ have been manufactured.
- Animal trials were completed with success.
- FDA 510(k) clearance for second indication is pending.
- Follow-on products to the Stone Sweeper™ are in the design stage.

Intellectual Property

Fossa has one issued patent and two patents pending. The issued patent, 6,214,037 "Radially Expanding Stent," covers ureteral stents that expand to hold a passageway open. Our patents pending cover the design and procedure of stone removal, including the baskets, in more detail. Prior art is covered in the issued patent. International patents are pending, and two more patents are being written.

> Important to highlight intellectual property as this is the basis of the company's competitive advantage.

Financial Highlights

The table below summarizes Fossa's five-year forecast of revenues and net earnings.

($ millions)	2002	2003	2004	2005	2006
REVENUES	0	1.0	4.5	11.5	27.0
COST OF GOODS	0	(0.3)	(1.0)	(2.5)	(5.9)
EXPENSES	(0.7)	(1.7)	(2.7)	(5.7)	(12.3)
NET EARNINGS	(0.7)	(0.9)	0.8	3.2	8.8

Capital Needs

> Highlighting that company has raised equity capital shows potential investors that others believe in its prospects.

Fossa has raised $425K and is currently looking for $3.7M. The first $425K is being used for prototype manufacturing, lab/animal testing, and the 510(k) clearance process for Fossa's first product, the Stone Sweeper. To use its funds most effectively, Fossa will contract with outside vendors for manufacturing, testing, and distribution. The remaining funds will be used to help prepare the company for its first product launch and develop second-generation products. The most likely exit for investors would be through an acquisition.

> This statement needs some further clarification. Who is likely to acquire Fossa and why?

Use of Investment (000)

> Table nicely lays out how the investment will be used.

Production Run		**$ 270**
Sales and Marketing		**$ 940**
- salaries	$490	
- promotion	$150	
- travel	$120	
- doctor support	$180	
R&D		**$ 450**
- salaries	$275	
- prototypes/test	$130	
- travel	$ 45	

(continues)

Use of Investment (000) continued

General and Administration expenses	**$ 340**
Future Product Development	**$1400**
Contingencies	**$ 300**
TOTAL	**$3700**

Team

> Team has deep experience, and the bios do a good job of highlighting that expertise.

> Provides overview of why the team is well suited to pursue project.

Fossa's management team has extensive experience in designing, marketing and selling medical devices. The team includes

- Gloria Ro Kolb, President, has engineering degrees from MIT and Stanford University and an MBA from Babson College. She has designed and launched over forty-five medical products for leading health-care companies such as Johnson & Johnson and was a design engineer for The Gillette Company.

> Highlights record of success in medical device field.

- Mike Kansas,[1] VP of Engineering, has led multinational, multi-million-dollar projects designing and manufacturing innovative medical products for companies such as Johnson & Johnson. He has guided over fifty products from design through FDA clearance and holds five patents.

> Suggests that team has experience at managing large organizations. Implies that Fossa has vision of strong growth.

- James Glenn, VP of Sales and Marketing, has over sixteen years of experience in medical sales, marketing, managing, developing plans, and growing sales.

> Quantifying how much he has grown sales would add further credibility.

- Dennis Jones, MD., Chief Medical Adviser, is a surgeon at Brigham & Women's Hospital in Boston. He has degrees from Princeton University and Harvard Medical School.

> Having a potential customer, and influencer, as an adviser strengthens your credibility.

- Jean-Paul Cormier, Ph.D., Board Member, managed Technomed, an ESWL machine company, and helped design laser lithotripsy devices. He is a cofounder of two other medical device companies, with one in the cardiovascular area.

> Should tell the reader what top ranking means. Best hospital? Most profitable? What?

- Petter Thomas, Board Member, has been President and CEO of Boston Hospital for the past nine years. He has consistently led the hospital to top rankings.

> Pointing out one or two key accomplishments adds credibility. Those 30 years of experience could have been in low-level positions.

- Andrew Martin, Ph.D., Adviser, has worked with the Pharmaceutical and Medical Device Industry for the last 30 years in the fields of product, business, and portfolio development.

[1]All names besides Gloria's have been disguised.

4

Sample Presentation

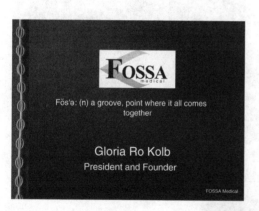

FOSSA

Fōs'ə: (n) a groove, point where it all comes together

Gloria Ro Kolb
President and Founder

FOSSA Medical

Fossa is Ready to Grab Large Markets

1. *Large, profitable Markets ⇒ Underserved*

2. *Innovative Products that can Serve*
   - Kidney Stone Sweeper is first out of five
   - Capture attention of doctors/leaders

3. *Building a Quick and Nimble Company*
   - FDA full market approval
   - Issued patents
   - Strong Team
   - Raising $3.5M

FOSSA Medical

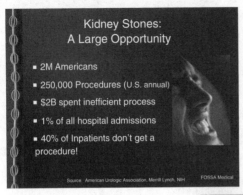

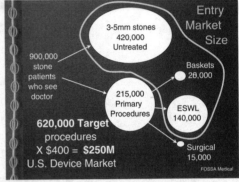

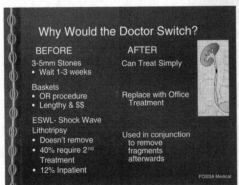

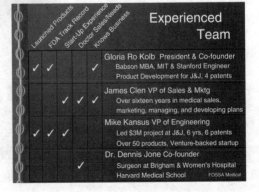

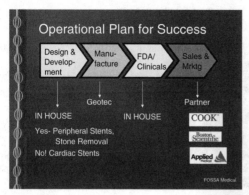

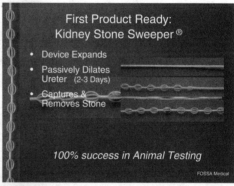

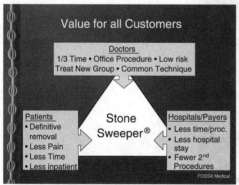

Competition Lacks Full Product Line

	Ureteral Stents	Basket Retrieval	Device w/ ESWL
FOSSA	X	X	X
Boston Scientific	X	X	
BARD	X	X	
Cook	X	X	
ACMI	X	X	

Competitors= Potential Acquirers

Source: Medical Data International   FOSSA Medical

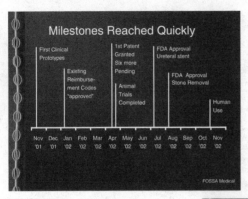

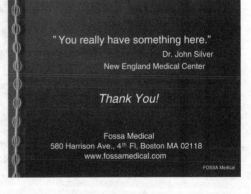

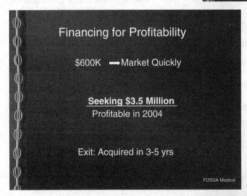

Index

Note: Boldface numbers indicate illustrations.

Dubinsky, Donna, 13
due diligence efforts, 58, 150
Dun and Bradstreet, 124
Dun's One Million Dollar Premium,
66
Dun's Principal International Business,
66

educational background of
entrepreneurs, 3
email/e–letters, in advertising and
promotions, 90
emotional vs. rational response in
marketing, 79–80, **80**
employees, staffing plan for, 100, **100**
energy, 14
Enron, 62F, 62
Entrepreneurship Quotient (EQ),
34–35
entrepreneurs, 1–24, 1
age of, 3
American, 2–10
business planning and, 4, 11–12
commitment in, 14
dot com boom/bust and, lessons for,
6–10
educational background of, 3
energy and, 14
Entrepreneurship Quotient (EQ)
and, 34–35
financing for, 7–9
"first mover's advantage" concept
and, 9–10
Global Entrepreneurship Model
(GEM) project and, 2
growth of business and, 5
initial public offerings (IPOs) and, 5,
7–8
knowledge in, 12–13
learning curve for, 4
money vs. personal achievement in,
11
nascent, 2, 3–4
networking and, 13–14
new business owners as, 2–3
number of, in U.S., 1–2
opportunity and, 15–23, **18**
passion in, 14–15
self-analysis for, 10–15

success in, keys to, 15–16
success rates for, 2, 3–6
survivor rates for, 5
sustainable organizations and, 4–6
time investment by, 14, 35
Timmons Model of, 2, 15–23, **16**
venture capital and, 5–6, 7–8
Zach's Star of Success for, 12–15,
12
entry and growth strategy, 77
estimating, in financing, financial
management, 122–125
ethics, 62F
eToys, 8
executive summary, 43, 51, **52–55**
expanded summary, 43
external members of team, 105–107

Factiva, 66
family-owned businesses, 10
Federal Express, 44, 45
financial information, 55
financial management (*See* financing;
resource/financial management)
financial plan (*See* financing, financial
management)
financial projections, 11f
financial ratios, 124
financing, financial management (*See
also* offering plan), 7–9, 18–19,
39–40, 121–143, **126–142**
accountants for, 121
actuals in, 126, **127**
assets and liabilities in, 134
availability and timing of, 114,
116–117
balance sheet in, 121, 125, 134,
141–142
bootstrapping, 19
burn rate and, 114
cash flow statement in, 121, 125,
134, **135–140**
conservative estimate methods in,
122
conserve your equity (CYE) in, 19
cost of goods sold (COGS) in, 128
critical risks analysis and, 114
description/explanation of financials
for, 126